CONTENTS

SKILL BUILDERS by Jane Vogel

PROBLEM SOLVERS by Carol Smith

Skill Builders and Problem Solvers

Jane Vogel and Carol Smith

David C. Cook Publishing Co.
Elgin, Illinois/Weston, Ontario

SNAP SESSIONS: Skill Builders and Problem Solvers

PUBLISHED BY
David C. Cook Publishing Co.
850 N. Grove Ave., Elgin, IL 60120
Cable address: DCCOOK

DESIGNED BY
Tabb Associates

INTERIOR ILLUSTRATIONS BY
Keith Locke

COVER ILLUSTRATION BY
Gary Locke

Printed in U.S.A.

ISBN: 0-7814-5051-9

Are You Too Busy to Read This Introduction?

It's 5:30 on a Sunday night. You're panicking. Your next youth group meeting is just 30 minutes away—and you aren't ready! In fact, you've been so busy this week that you haven't really gotten *anything* together for this meeting!

Sweat pops from your forehead as you flip through the programming resources on your shelf. But the typical meeting plan you find there requires you to gather a crate of eggplants and a parachute, cut 50 index cards into two-inch squares, and round up a panel of guest speakers. There's no time for that!

Some plans on your shelf are simpler, but require you to photocopy reproducible student sheets—and you don't have quick access to a copier. And since your group's meeting outside, you don't have a chalkboard, either.

What are you going to do? If only there were some books of *really* easy-to-prepare youth meetings, sessions that you could read and put together at top speed!

Now there are! The *Snap Sessions* series is designed specifically for busy youth workers—which includes practically all of us!

The Simple Truth

What's so great about a Snap Session? Simple: It's simple!

• To lead a Snap Session, you *never need more than Bibles, pencils, paper, and a household object!* There's no photocopying or cutting or pasting or rehearsing, either!

• It's easy to grasp each session plan at a glance. Instructions to you are in regular type; things you could say to the group are in bold type; suggested answers are in parentheses.

• Despite the ease of preparation, meetings are full-length (45-60 minutes) and full-strength (creative, active, and relating the Bible to kids' lives).

• If you have extra preparation time, you can dress the meeting up with optional, more involved activities listed at the end of each session.

We could go on and on about *Snap Sessions*—but we know you don't have time. Grab one of the 30 sessions that follow and get going! Your group members are ready for a great meeting—and you're about to give them one!

—Randy Southern, Series Editor

DATE USED

How to Study

BIG IDEA

Almost everybody prefers relaxing over hard work. But if you follow God's advice about laziness and diligence, you'll reap the benefits in less stress and better grades.

BIBLE INPUT

Selected Proverbs

BRING:

Bibles
Pencils
Paper

1 Play "Can't Keep Up"

Sit in a circle and assign everyone a number, starting with 1 and going around the circle in order. Player #1 starts a rhythm by patting his or her knees twice, then clapping hands twice, and continuing this pattern. Once all the other players have caught the pace and joined in, Player #1 calls, in rhythm with the clapping, "1, 1, 5, 5" (or any other number in the group). Without missing a beat, Player #5 must call "5, 5, 3, 3" (or any other number), and so on until a player misses a beat in calling. That player moves to the low end of the circle and everyone with a lower number moves up, getting a new number to remember and call. Player #1 always starts the new round and sets the pace. The goal is to get to be Player #1.

2 Identify Study Pressures

Move one place to the right (even if it means sitting on someone's lap) if you've ever . . .

- **felt like you couldn't keep up with the pace a teacher was setting in class.**
- **felt like you were forgetting the main points in a subject.**
- **felt like your grade depended on beating out your classmates.**
- **felt like you'd never make it to the top of the class.**
- **felt like you couldn't get everything done that your teachers expected of you.**
- **felt like you were going to slip up and see your grades drop if you weren't really, really careful.**

3 A Fool versus a Wise Person

Even smart people and good students feel the pressure to succeed in school. And even people who have a hard time in school can do things to make school a little easier for themselves. The Book of Proverbs was written by the smartest man who ever lived, King Solomon. In it, he gives some very practical advice about how to learn.

Divide into two groups. Assign the following verses and ask one group to jot down the characteristics of a wise person, the other group to summarize the characteristics of a fool.

- Proverbs 10:8: The wise in heart accept commands, but a chattering fool comes to ruin.
- Proverbs 12:1: Whoever loves discipline loves knowledge, but he who hates correction is stupid.

• Proverbs 12:24: Diligent hands will rule, but laziness ends in slave labor.

• Proverbs 14:23: All hard work brings a profit, but mere talk leads only to poverty.

• Proverbs 17:24: A discerning man keeps wisdom in view, but a fool's eyes wander to the ends of the earth.

Have each group pick a member to be their "demonstration model," then give a sales pitch using the characteristics noted to describe their model as the "Ultimate Wise Guy" or the "Perfect Fool."

4 Study DOs & DON'Ts

Look again at the characteristics the groups wrote down, and discuss a practical way each verse relates to study habits. Ask each person to jot down the ideas in two columns, one for DOs and one for DON'Ts. For example:

• Proverbs 10:8 (DO follow through on assignments and instructions; DON'T waste class time and study time talking with your friends.)

• Proverbs 12:1 (DO be disciplined enough to make studying a priority; DON'T give up and refuse to learn from your mistakes.)

• Proverbs 12:24 (DO keep up with your homework; DON'T be lazy or you'll end up working like a slave right before papers or exams are due.)

• Proverbs 14:23 (DO work hard on your schoolwork, and it will pay off; DON'T expect to get anywhere by complaining about it .)

• Proverbs 17:24 (DO keep your goal in mind and stay focused while you're studying; DON'T let distractions like TV, snacking, or phone calls interrupt your studying.)

Ask kids to share other study techniques that work for them (setting aside a regular time to study every day; reviewing or rewriting class notes each week; asking for help before you get behind; rewarding yourself by seeing friends or watching a favorite show after your study time; etc.), or things they've learned to avoid. Encourage kids to add these ideas to their lists.

5 Grade Your Study Habits

Give kids a few minutes to evaluate how well they accomplish the DOs on the list and how well they avoid the DON'Ts. Ask them to pick one or two suggestions to put into practice this week, and have them write out specifically how they will do so, if appropriate. (For example, "I will rewrite my Chemistry notes every day," or, "I will study for 30 minutes right after school.") Encourage kids to post their DOs and DON'Ts lists where they will see them while they do their homework.

Optional Extras

1. *Test Panel.* Ask volunteers to test the suggestions developed in this session for a week or more, then report back to the group on how well they worked.

2. *Study Center.* Set a time and place where group members can come once a month or once a week to study. Invite adults or teachers who can help with homework questions. Follow the study time with a fun activity.

3. *Exercise in Concentration.* Bring a portable cassette stereo player, a king-size bag of M & M's, and a bowl to this session (but keep these out of sight). Also make arrangements with two people to interrupt your meeting at a set time. Tell group members that you want them to practice their memorization skills, and ask them to turn in their Bibles to a rather obscure passage such as II Chronicles 31; Ezekiel 25:1-14; or Zephaniah 1:1-13. Explain that they have five minutes to memorize the passage. Do make sure each kid has a Bible. Give kids a few seconds to get situated, and then do everything you can do to break their concentration. Turn on the stereo and pump up the volume. Open the bag of M & M's, pour the candy into the bowl, and pass it around. Stage a coughing fit. For the grand finale, your two cohorts should make a grand entrance into your meeting place, and then the three of you should carry on a loud inane conversation. Meanwhile, keep shouting the time remaining. By the time the five minutes are up, kids will have caught on to your tactics. Do ask if anyone memorized the passage; then use this setup as a lead-in to a discussion about how easy it is to be distracted when you need to concentrate.

DATE USED

Tips for Taking Tests

BIG IDEA

Some practical tips can help you next time you take a test. But don't forget that grades aren't everything.

BIBLE INPUT

I Samuel 16:1-13

BRING:

Bibles
Pencils
Paper
Tray of assorted objects

1 Test Powers of Observation

Ask a volunteer (someone from your church, but not part of your group) to carry a tray covered with a variety of items past each person. Say: **Look closely, because you will be tested on your powers of observation.** Have the volunteer leave the room and stay outside while you hand out paper and pencils and give the following test:

1. Who was carrying the tray?
2. What color are his or her eyes?
3. What color is his or her hair?
4. Describe the color and style of his or her clothes.
5. Describe any jewelry, glasses, etc., that he or she was wearing.
6. Is this person taller or shorter than you?

Invite the volunteer back into the room and see who answered the most questions correctly and completely.

Was this a fair test? (Not really; kids were led to think that they would be tested on the objects on the tray, not on the person carrying the tray.)

What would have helped you to do better on the "test"? (Knowing what to look for, what to study.)

Have you ever taken a real test in school where you felt as if you had studied all the wrong things?

2 Test Test-Taking Tips

Have kids line up in single file.

I'm going to read some tips for preparing for and taking tests. If you have tried this tip, take one step to the right. If you haven't tried it, take one step to the left.

After each tip, ask one or two of those who have tried it whether or not the tip was effective.

- **Prepare for a test by writing an outline of your class notes.**
- **Quickly read through the whole test before you begin answering questions.**
- **Organize your answers to essay questions by jotting down a quick outline on scrap paper or in the margin.**
- **On multiple-choice tests, stick with your first response; it's usually right.**
- **Don't leave any questions blank; you might pick up a few points with a good guess.**
- **If you have to guess on a multiple-choice test, try to eliminate as many of the choices as you can by looking for those that are clearly wrong.**
- **Remember that the two extremes in a multiple-choice answer (like the highest and lowest in a range of answers) are least likely to be correct.**

• On true/false tests, look for words like "never" and "always"; they usually indicate a false statement.

• Watch out for details in true/false statements; if any part of the statement is false, the whole thing is false.

Invite kids to offer other tips that they have used and found effective.

3 Practice Your Test-taking Skills

Divide into teams and ask each team to write a five-question quiz on I Samuel 16:1-13. Specify that at least one question be essay, one multiple choice, and one true/false. Encourage the teams to write questions that can be answered by applying the test-taking tips. (For example, a multiple-choice question might ask whether Jesse had 4, 6, 8, or 10 sons. The tip about eliminating the two extremes would apply.) When the teams are done, have them exchange quizzes and work as a team to answer the questions. When everyone is done, share answers and talk about how the test-taking tips applied.

4 Apply What You Learn

It's easy to cram for a test and then forget everything you've learned as soon as the test is over. It's harder to keep in mind that our priority should be on learning, not just on getting good grades. Let's talk about what we learned from the passage you just took a test on. Briefly discuss the story and characters presented in I Samuel 16:1-13.

If Samuel, not God, had been "grading" Jesse's sons, which son would he have given an A? (Probably Eliab [vs. 6].)

What is more important to God than how well we measure up to external standards? (What He sees in our hearts [vs. 7].)

How does this truth relate to your grades? (We shouldn't brag or feel superior if we're good students; we don't need to feel worthless if we have a hard time with school; our worth in God's eyes is based on our relationship to Him, not on our grades.)

Optional Extras

1. *Tip List*. Photocopy the test-taking tips listed in Step 2 and provide them as a resource for students to use in Step 3 and to refer to when they study for real tests.

2. *Teacher Talk*. Invite teachers to talk with the group about how they decide what material to ask on tests and what they think would help students prepare.

3. *Heart Awards*. At this meeting or throughout the course of the year, stage an "awards ceremony" or "honors convocation" to celebrate and recognize kids' achievements in spiritual growth or Christian service. Be as specific as possible in identifying individuals' spiritual gifts. Help them build self-concepts based on more than just academic success or failure.

4. *Testing, One-Two-Three*. In advance (before Step 1), have kids fill out a simple questionnaire, and then develop a test around their answers. You could hand out the test between Steps 1 and 2.

   Give a few volunteers calculators to figure out the answers and then supply some multiple-choice answers. Make sure to use some of the test-taking tips.

   Here are some sample questions.

   1. What is the average age of our group?
   2. How many people receive an allowance?
   3. What is the favorite flavor of ice cream among our group?
   4. What is the average number of pets in this group.
   5. What is the amount of time people watched TV yesterday
   6. What is the average amount of time people spent studying yesterday?

DATE USED

Making a Good Impression

BIG IDEA

The best way to make a good impression is to focus on the other person, not yourself.

BIBLE INPUT

I Peter 4:8
I Corinthians 13:4-7
Philippians 2:3, 4
I John 4:18, 19

BRING:

Bibles
Pencils
Paper
Paper grocery sacks

1 Make Masks

Ask kids to brainstorm situations in which they would want to make a good impression. (First date, job interview, tryouts or auditions, etc.) Hand out pencils and paper sacks and instruct everyone to make a mask someone might wear to put his or her "best face forward" in one of those situations. (If the bags have writing on them, have the kids carefully turn them inside out.) Let them be as straightforward or creative as they wish. Some may simply wish to draw a face, others may want to put notes of explanation ("sincere smile, wax-free ears") by the features.

Have them put on their masks and introduce themselves as the characters they have illustrated, highlighting their best features to make a good impression.

2 List Ways to Mask Your Faults

Take the masks off and discuss: **What would you think of someone who tried to impress you by telling you all of his good points?** (He's a phony; he's self-centered; he must have something to hide; he's too insecure to let me see the real him.)

You can't hide behind a mask, but you can do something to cover up your faults—not in a sneaky way, but in a good way. Invite a volunteer to read I Peter 4:8 and discuss how love "covers over a multitude of sins." (If you love someone, you are willing to overlook their faults; if you are committed to acting in a loving way, your own sinful selfishness will be more under control; if others know you are a loving person, they'll be more willing to overlook your faults.)

Turn your bag over and draw a circle the size of your face on this side. Let's come up with specific ways to show love to one another and write down the suggestions anywhere outside of the circle. After your kids have given ideas, turn to I Corinthians 13:4-7 and compare the suggestions with this familiar description of love. Have kids add any new ideas from the passage on their bags.

We can find a good summary of how to get relationships off to a good start in Philippians 2:3, 4. Read the passage and discuss how thinking of others rather than yourself can help you get relationships off to a positive start. (You won't be so nervous or self-conscious, because you're not worried about making a good impression. Instead, you're focused on the needs and interests of the other person.)

3 List Inner Needs of Others

To put other people first, you have to be aware of what they need and want. Let's brainstorm some of the needs most people have inside, and write them on

the insides of our bags. (Need to be liked, accepted, listened to, respected, to feel good about themselves, etc. People also need to feel safe in their relationships.)

4 Good and Bad Impressions

Ask volunteers to roleplay the following situations, first the way someone would act if he or she were thinking only of his or her need to impress, then how someone would act who was thinking first of the other person's needs.

- sitting next to a guy or girl you like on the bus to a field trip
- on a first date
- meeting the parents of your date
- at a job application or interview
- in the lunchroom with group of kids you'd like to know

Add other situations that kids mentioned in Step 1.

5 Unmask Your Fears

It's not so hard to put the other person first when we're just practicing like this, but when you're in a real situation it isn't always as easy. What fears or doubts could make you self-conscious instead of other-conscious? (Fear that I won't know what to say; that I'll say or do something stupid; that the other person will snub me; etc.) As kids give suggestions, have them write them in the circle they drew earlier.

We can reduce some of these fears by practicing our conversational skills, making sure we use mouthwash, and things like that. But to really get rid of fear, we come back to a familiar cure. Read I John 4:18, 19.

Why can we have the kind of love that "drives out fear"? (Because God first loved us [vs. 19]. We don't have to worry about impressing Him, so we can be free to share that love with others.)

Ask group members to tear out the circle with their fears written in it and throw it away as a symbol of getting rid of their fears. Let them put on the bags, with their faces showing through the hole they have just torn. Their faces will be framed by the practical ideas for putting others first.

Instead of hiding behind masks to make a good impression, we can let our real selves show if we're willing to focus on the other person instead of ourselves. And that will make a real impression!

Optional Extras

1. *Plaster Impressions*. Let your kids make a literal impression in plaster of paris with their feet (like outside Grauman's Chinese Theater in Hollywood), then have others etch in qualities they see in them. Make a "walk of the stars" and affirm your kids for the good impressions they are already making. Read Philippians 2:14, 15, where Paul says we can "shine like stars." Point out that this promise comes shortly after the passage about putting others first.

2. *Expert Opinions*. Before the meeting, survey your kids to find out where they most want to make a good impression. Invite a panel of appropriate people (other kids, employers, parents, etc.) to talk about what impresses them.

DATE USED

Getting Parents to Trust You

BIG IDEA Trust is based on a foundation of responsible actions. Most parents won't give you trust until you earn it.

BIBLE INPUT Genesis 25:24-28
Genesis 27:1-35

BRING:
Bibles
Pencils
Paper
Old bed sheet

1 Take a Trust Walk

Have each kid tear a blindfold from an old sheet, then do a variation of the popular "trust walk." Have the first guides lead their blindfolded partners very carefully, but when they trade places, secretly indicate to the new guides that they are to lead their partners into obstacles—without hurting them, of course.

When the walk is over, ask:

Did it get easier or harder to trust your guide as the walk went on? (Easier for the first blindfolded set as they realized their guides were not going to let them get hurt. Harder for the second set as they realized their guides were untrustworthy.)

How did you feel when your guide deliberately let you run into things? (Bruised; surprised; betrayed because I didn't let him get hurt.)

If we played another blindfold game now, would you trust your partner?

Encourage kids to express their opinions of why or why not they would trust their guides for one more round.

In terms of your relationship with your parent(s), do you see yourself more as a guide who can be counted on, or as one who doesn't live up to their trust?

How do you think your parents see you?

2 Act Out Jacob and Esau's Story

Read Genesis 25:24-28 to introduce the characters in this story, then recruit four volunteers to play the parts of Isaac, Esau, Rebekah, and Jacob. Ask them to pantomime their roles as you read Genesis 27:1-35 aloud. Encourage the rest of the group to cheer and boo whomever they think are heroes and villains.

Who was the good guy in this story? Who was the bad guy? (Do kids know that Jacob, the "bad guy" in this story, is actually a "hero" in the larger story of the Bible? God chooses Jacob, not Esau, to be the father of the tribes of Israel [Jacob's new name]. Just as Jacob proved untrustworthy, so can even the "good kids" in your group, which may be one reason parents are hesitant to trust them.)

If you were Isaac, would you trust Jacob after this experience? Why or why not?

Do you think Jacob had an excuse for what he did? (Kids may argue that Jacob was only obeying his mother. Point out that this sort of influence is what parents have in mind when they say, "I trust you, but not those kids at the party, the other drivers on the road, etc.")

In your opinion, did either Jacob or Esau deserve to be trusted? (Actually, both brothers were schemers. They weren't beneath playing up to the particular parent who favored them.)

3 Test Your Trustworthiness

Questions about blessings and hairy arms probably aren't big issues for you and your parents. Let's list some areas where parents do have a hard time giving you the kind of trust you want. (Suggestions may include: driving privileges, curfews, choice of entertainment, etc.)

Distribute paper and pencils. Say: **I'm going to read two situations about the issue of trust between kids and parents. Choose one of the situations and write your own ending to it. Here's the first situation.**

Gina's parents had a rule: no R-rated movies. Some of Gina's friends from school wanted to go to the city's international film festival. Gina's parents already gave her permission to go. Now her mom wanted to know what kinds of movies Gina planned on watching.

"Films," Gina corrected her mother. "These are artistic films."

"Nudity is nudity," replied Gina's mother. "No R-rated movies, honey."

Gina knew that a lot of foreign films had an R-rating, but wasn't there an exception to every rule?

Now the second situation.

Nathan's parents always wanted Nathan and his sister to fill up the tank of gas whenever they used the car. His parents worried about them being stranded on a lonely, dark highway. This evening, Nathan's dad gave him twenty dollars and said, "I didn't have time to put gas in. Do it on your way to the party."

"No problem," Nathan said. When he got in the car, Nathan checked the fuel gauge. He had enough gas to get to the party. He'd stop on his way home.

On the way, Nathan picked up a few of his friends, and they stopped by the store for food. Without thinking, Nathan paid for the food with the twenty his dad gave him.

After a few hours at the party, Nathan and friends went cruising. No big deal . . . until they ran out of gas just as Nathan's curfew ran out too. Nathan pounded his head against the steering wheel. "I'm dead," he groaned.

Encourage kids to come up with creative resolutions, not simply pat answers. Call on volunteers to read their endings. Afterwards, discuss whether or not the characters proved their trustworthiness.

Before moving on to the next step, ask kids to grade their trustworthiness on a scale of 5 (I never do any of these things parents are afraid of) to 1 (I do these things every time I'm in this situation).

4 Plan to Prove Yourself

Have kids choose partners and talk about ways they could show their parents they are willing to demonstrate their trustworthiness in specific areas such as curfews, driving privileges, and choice of entertainment.

Instruct them to tear their blindfolds into three long strips, write an action step on each strip, and braid the three strips. Encourage them to wear the braid like a friendship bracelet or anklet to remind them to carry out their plans this week.

Optional Extras

1. *Negotiation Role Plays*. What if parents never give kids a chance to prove their trustworthiness? Discuss ways to respectfully negotiate terms and compromises, then roleplay similar situations.

2. *Parent Forum*. Invite parents to join this meeting. Have them make a list of top ways kids lose parents' trust and use this list in Step 3. Have teams of parents and kids work together to develop a plan for earning and giving trust.

DATE USED

How to Get a Job

BIG IDEA

To get a job, you need to find openings, be realistic about your abilities, then put your best foot forward. You can start now becoming the kind of person that employers want to hire.

BIBLE INPUT

Titus 2:9, 10
Colossians 3:22-25

BRING:

Bibles
Pencils
Paper
Masking tape

1 Find Job Openings

Hand out paper and pencils. Form small teams or let kids compete individually to list the greatest number of ways to find out about job openings for teenagers. (See signs in the window; check with school counselor or placement center; hear from a friend; etc.) Allow about two minutes, then score as follows:

- 10 points for every way the group agrees is valid;
- 20 points for every valid response that no one else listed.

For the kids who already have jobs, you could ask them to be the judges, and let them have the final say on the validity of the teams' answers.

Repeat the contest, asking this time for the longest list of jobs available to teenagers in your area (whether or not those jobs are currently open). Be sure kids list specific places, like "McDonald's," not general categories, like "fast food joints."

2 Match Skills to the Openings

Divide up the jobs listed in Step 1 among pairs of kids. Ask each pair to write out brief "job descriptions" listing what they think the requirements for holding that job would be. Discuss them as a group and add any other requirements the group thinks of.

Now pick two or three jobs that you think you would like to do. Explain to your partner why you meet the requirements. Be sure to include in your considerations how you would get to work and what hours you would be available. Encourage kids to be realistic about their extracurricular schedules.

3 Create the Ideal Employee

When you go to apply for a job, an employer is going to want to know more than whether or not you can make change or run a cash register. Your employer will want to know about your character too—what kind of person you are. What are some qualities or characteristics you would look for if you were hiring someone? (Honesty, trustworthiness, friendliness, getting to work on time, clean appearance, etc.)

Do you think an employer has the right to expect all these things from you? (Some may say yes—if she is paying me, she can set the requirements. Others may say no—as long as I do the job, it's nobody's business how I dress or wear my hair.)

The Bible gives us some guidelines about attitudes toward employers. Ask volunteers to read aloud Titus 2:9, 10 and Colossians 3:22-25.

Sometimes people call their bosses "slave-drivers," but some people in New

Testament times really did have slave-drivers. In fact, there were slaves who had become Christians. And as Christians, these slaves had to approach things differently. They were to obey their masters, to try to please them, not to talk back to them, and not to steal from them.

• **How do you think the Christian slaves felt about these instructions?** As kids express their thoughts, you might want to mention that in Roman society, slaves had no legal rights, and their fate was in their masters' hands. Paul didn't condone slavery nor did he call for a revolt. Instead, Paul wanted both slaves and masters to live out Christian principles in their relationships, attempting to change the institution from the inside.

• **What do you think was the rationale behind these instructions?** (Now that the slaves had come to Christ, everything they did—sinful actions excluded—was for the Lord. Ultimately, they were serving the Lord, not just their human masters. Also, the slaves would be able to influence their masters for Christ.)

• **How do these instructions apply to us as employees today?** (The attitude of respect for authority remains the same. We can work even under difficult conditions if we remember that our responsibility is ultimately to God. And at least we can go home after work—the New Testament slaves never got a break.)

Form small groups to "create" the ideal employee. Instruct them to tear labels out of paper and write a different characteristics of a good employee on each. Then have them tape the labels on one of their team members. (For example, good grooming could be illustrated by a label near the mouth reading, "No bad breath.") Line up the labeled kids and let others vote for the one most likely to get hired.

4 *Take the First Step*

If you're serious about finding a job, the next step is up to you. Start finding out what jobs are available. Figure out which ones you could do. Then put your best foot forward and show that you are the kind of person worth hiring.

Even if you're not serious about a job right now, some day you will be. Start now by becoming the kind of person that others want to hire—not just in skills and grooming, but especially in character and attitude.

Optional Extras

1. *Job Scavenger Hunt.* If you have drivers and cars available, give teams a fixed amount of time to come back with the longest list of real job openings available to teenagers (including the position, company, and location). They may drive around, phone around, look through want ads, etc. Give a geographical radius appropriate to your group. Compile the lists of job openings and make them available to group members looking for work.

2. *Help Wanted.* Do some legwork before the meeting and compile a list of appropriate job openings, based on information from newspapers, signs you see, etc. Make these available to those who are looking for work.

3. *Job Fair.* Hold a job fair with prospective employers from your church (including those looking for yardwork, etc.)

4. *Junior High Adaptation.* For junior highers, focus on creative options for earning money. Share ideas on the old standbys like baby-sitting, lawn mowing, and paper routes that are familiar to adults but new to kids who have never done them.

5. *Training Video.* Many personnel or human resources departments have short videos for new employees that stress the importance of eye contact, grooming, promptness, etc. Check with church members or at your work about borrowing a video for your group.

DATE USED

How to Break a Bad Habit

BIG IDEA

The best way to break a bad habit is to replace it with a good one. And Christ will help us overcome both big sins and bad habits.

BIBLE INPUT

Colossians 3:8-14
Romans 6:6, 7

BRING:

Bibles
Pencils
Paper
Package of nails
Empty pop bottle

1 Play "Biting Your Nails"

Forms teams to compete in this nail-biting version of drop the clothespin in the bottle. Have each team stand in a single-file line, and place a pop bottle about four feet to six feet from each line. Give each person a nail, and explain the game as follows. **When it's your turn, bite down on the nail, and with the nail still in your mouth, race to the bottle and try to drop it into the bottle. You'll have three tries to get it in. Ready? First person in line, bite the nail.** Remind players that good aim is as important as speed in this relay! Declare the team that got the most nails in the jar the winner. Its prize? They may keep all of the nails.

2 Identify Bad Habits

Have you ever known anyone who had the bad habit of biting his or her nails? What kinds of things did they do to try to stop? (Parents put bad-tasting stuff on the nails; bought nail polish to use when the nails were grown out; wore gloves; etc.)

What are some other common bad habits? (Overeating; picking your nose; almost always being late; watching TV even when there is nothing good on; putting off doing your homework or other chores; gossiping; leaving dirty clothes lying around; etc.)

Can you think of ways that some bad habits could eventually lead to serious consequences? (A habit of messiness could make parents angry, get you grounded, alienate a college roommate or a spouse some day. If you're often late you could miss important information in class and get a bad grade; you could lose a date because the person thinks you're standing him or her up; someday you could be fired for not being at work on time.) Allow kids to have fun coming up with extreme examples as well as realistic ones.

Not every bad habit leads to serious consequences. Some habits are just annoying to others, and some, like biting your nails, probably don't bother anybody but the person who does it. But even "little" bad habits can be hard to break.

3 Nail Down Your Bad Habit

Hand out paper and pencils. Give kids a few minutes to think of a specific bad habit they want to break. Then ask them to list the following down the left side of the paper:

1. **What habit you want to break** (Example: Pigging out on junk food.)
2. **Where you usually do it** (In front of the TV.)
3. **When you usually do it** (While watching TV before supper.)
4. **Why you do it or what triggers it** (I like to have something to do with my hands while I watch my show, I'm hungry, I'm bored.)

Some kids may be embarrassed about their bad habits; make sure they know that they will not have to share what they've written with the group.

4 Discover a Solution

If you've already tried breaking this bad habit before, you know how hard it can be. Most people can't just say, "I won't do this anymore," and quit. Usually it takes more than willpower to break a bad habit; it takes a plan of action. Let's see what God suggests.

Ask one volunteer to read Colossians 3:8, 9 and another to read verses 10-14. (In many Bible versions, verse 10 is the completion of the sentence in verse 9. Don't worry about changing readers in the middle of a sentence; you want your kids to see clearly where the contrast starts.)

What everyday physical action does Paul use to describe a spiritual action? (Taking something old off and putting something new on. He compares bad actions and good actions to old and new clothes.)

Suppose you had an important meeting—a job interview or a conference with the principal. And you didn't want to go in your grubby old jeans you wore to mow the lawn. So you took off all your old clothes, but you didn't put any new ones on. Would you be any better off? (Of course not.) **Suppose you didn't have any other clothes. What would you do?** (Put the old ones back on or go get new ones.)

Help kids see how this clothes analogy applies to bad habits. If you try to "take off" a bad habit but don't have anything to put in its place, you'll probably end up slipping back into the old habit. Instead of leaving yourself vulnerable when you quit a habit, plan ahead and put something in its place—like planning ahead to have new clothes to replace the old.

What are some of the bad things this passage tells us to get rid of? (Anger, rage, malice, slander, filthy language, lying [vss. 8, 9].)

What are some of the good things we should replace them with? (Compassion, kindness, humility, gentleness, patience, forgiveness, love [vss. 12-14].)

These good things aren't second nature to us, but they are part of the new nature, the new life, we have in Christ. Christ wants to help us replace the old with the new, the bad with the good.

If replacing the bad with the good works for such serious things as spiritual values, do you think it might work for your bad habit? Remind kids to be realistic. This is not a magic formula but a guideline for commonsense living that will take some planning and discipline on their part.

5 Nail Down an Action Plan

Refer kids back to their papers where they described the bad habits they want to break. Instruct them to write the following questions on the right side of the page:

1. **What good thing you could do instead of the bad habit** (Sample answer: Instead of eating junk food I could eat carrots or something healthy.)

2. **How you could avoid the place or break the pattern of doing the bad habit at that place?** (I could watch fewer shows. I could ask my brother to nag me everytime he sees me taking food to the TV room.)

3. **How you could break the pattern of doing your bad habit at that time?** (Similar to above. Also, avoid watching TV before supper, when I'm hungry.)

4. **What else could meet the triggering need?** (I could keep my hands busy while I watch TV by brushing the dog, folding the laundry for Mom, doing craftwork, or just braiding strings together.)

Give everyone a nail and suggest they keep it as a reminder at the place where they are most likely to slip back into their bad habit.

6 Rely on Christ's Power

Breaking that bad habit is still going to take willpower. But if you believe in Jesus Christ you can have more than just willpower; you can have God's power.

Read Romans 6:6, 7. Hold up a nail and remind kids that Jesus was nailed to the cross to set us free from whatever enslaves us—big sins and little bad habits. Close with a prayer claiming that power.

Optional Extras

1. *Alternate Nail Relay*. Instead of dropping the nail into the bottle, have teams pass the nail from bare foot to bare foot.

2. *Object Lesson*. Illustrate the concept of "putting on" and "putting off" in Step 3 by asking a volunteer to walk across the room with a rope hobbling his or her ankles together. Then substitute an anklet for the hobble and discuss how sinful actions are like a ball and chain, but Christlike actions bring freedom.

3. *Mutual Accountability*. Let kids choose partners to be accountable to this week. Encourage them to check in with each other several times during the week to encourage each other in breaking their bad habits.

DATE USED

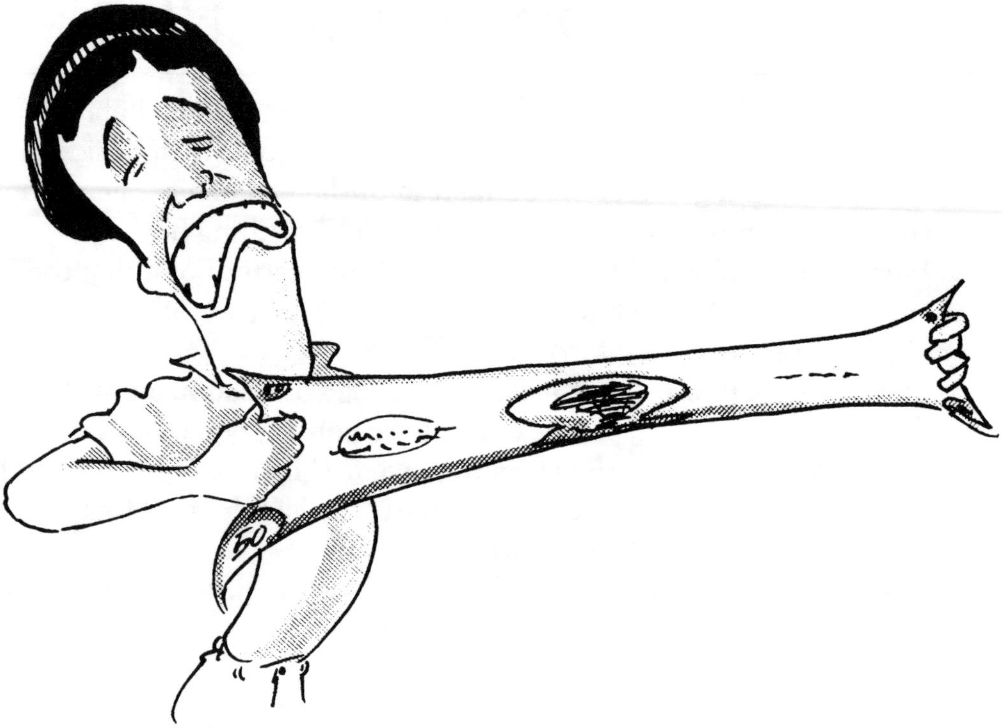

Making the Most of Your Money

BIG IDEA

To make the most of your money, you have to get your priorities straight. God wants us to give first to Him, then be responsible with what's left.

BIBLE INPUT

Proverbs 3:9, 10
Matthew 6:19-21

BRING:

Bibles
Pencils
Paper
Set of play money

1 Spend Play Money

Distribute play money in equal shares. Hand out paper and pencils and ask each kid to draw one item that would be desirable for teenagers (car, college tuition, great wardrobe, etc.). Don't allow more than one picture of the same item. Assign each picture a price that the kids' play money could cover (e.g., a down payment on a car, monthly savings toward college), set up the pictures around the room, and let kids "spend" their play money by putting it in front of the picture of the thing(s) they would buy.

When kids have "spent" all their money, count the money in front of each picture to see which item got the most buyers. Discuss what these purchases say about priorities. (Remember that kids were fantasizing about what they would like to own, so don't try to make them feel guilty for "spending" extravagantly.) Ask whether there are other valuable ways to spend money besides those pictured (gifts for friends, charity, church, necessities like lunch money or gas).

2 Discover God's Investment Plan

Read Proverbs 3:9, 10.

What does it mean to honor God with our wealth? (To use it in ways that please Him; to give some of our money for His work.)

How does this instruction apply to you if you're not wealthy? (You should still honor God with whatever money you do have.)

What do you think it meant to honor God with the firstfruits of the crop? (God's people were expected to give Him their very first portion when their crops were ready for harvest, before they took any for themselves.)

What does it mean to honor God with our firstfruits today? (Budget a portion of your earnings to give to church or charity; set aside that money before you spend it on anything else.)

What if you feel like you hardly have enough money as it is, without giving some for God's work? (God promises to reward His people when they make His work their first priority [vs. 10].)

Do you think the promise in verse 10 means that giving to God is a surefire investment scheme? (Our motivation in giving to God shouldn't be to get rich ourselves; some people who give faithfully still have financial difficulties; God does promise to reward us, but maybe it doesn't happen right away or the reward is not a material one.)

Read Matthew 6:19-21.

According to these verses, what could happen if you spend all your money buying "treasures" for yourself? (They could get stolen or destroyed.)

Have you ever had a prize possession that was ruined somehow? (Invite kids to tell what happened to their possessions, and how they felt when they discovered that these possessions had been ruined.)

What is the only "investment" with a guaranteed return? (Storing up treasures in heaven.) **How do you do this?** (Give your heart to God; give some of your money for God's work.) **What will be the reward?** (Eternal life; blessings like joy and contentment now.)

If you were going to summarize what these verses teach about money, what would you say is the first step toward making the most of your money? (Make your first priority "investing" in spiritual things by giving for God's work.)

3 Prioritize Your Expenses

Let's say you've made giving to God your first priority. You are pretty confident of those treasures in heaven, but you still have things you need and want to buy here and now.

Brainstorm things that kids need and things that kids want to buy. Include long-term goals like saving for college or a car. Ask kids to list their expenses for an average month, including necessities, discretionary spending, and any new savings or giving they want to start. Then have them number the expenses in order of priority.

Are your priorities in line with God's priorities? (Yes, if giving to God is at the top of the list and you are responsible about taking care of necessities. No, if you are wasting all your money on things that won't last.)

What if the money gives out before the list is done? (Delay lower priorities; look into ways of reducing costs; earn more money.)

4 Monitor Your Spending

Have kids draw up a chart listing their spending priorities down the left side of the page and the days of the week across the top. Encourage them to record how they spend their money this week and see what their spending says about their priorities.

Optional Extras

1. *Bargain Hunt.* Have each kid bring $1.00 for a bargain-hunting contest. Divide into teams of four and an adult helper, who is the designated driver on each team. Set a time limit and send them shopping. Make sure some of the items can be bought with coupons. Award a prize to the team with the lowest receipt. Give the items they bought to charity. If you don't want to send your kids out shopping, bring in some catalogs and have them do the same thing only mail order.

2. *Budget Review.* Together review your youth group budget, including sources of income and how the money is spent. What does your budget say about the group's priorities? Does the group spend all its money on itself?

3. *Group Giving.* Look into a group giving project like sponsoring a child, supporting a missionary, or giving regularly to a local food bank.

DATE USED

Handling Stress

BIG IDEA

Handle what you can one day at a time, and turn over what you can't handle to God.

BIBLE INPUT

Matthew 6:25-34
Psalm 42:11
Philippians 4:6, 7
Matthew 26:39

BRING:

Bibles
Pencils
Paper
Package of rubber bands

1 Stretch to the Breaking Point

Give each pair of kids a rubber band and have them compete to see which pair can stretch their rubber band the farthest.

Ask the winning pair: **What was the key to success in this contest?** (Knowing how far you could stretch without breaking the rubber band; not being afraid of getting snapped if the rubber band did break; having the biggest or most flexible rubber band; etc.)

Make the transition to the topic of stress with questions like these:

Can you think of a time when you felt that pressures and stress—about school, at home, with friends, or whatever—were stretching you out of shape like these rubber bands?

How did you know how far you could stretch your rubber bands? (You can sort of feel when it is getting ready to break; you can see it getting thinner and weaker; when it doesn't stretch easily, you've gone far enough; sometimes you only know by finding out you've stretched it too far.)

How do you know how much stress you can take? (You can feel it when you're getting to the breaking point; others can see that you're getting crabby and irritable; when you lose your flexibility, you've reached your limit; sometimes you find out only after you've taken on too much.)

2 Take a Stress Test

Hand out papers and pencils. Ask: **What are some of the stresses kids you know face?** (Pressure to do well in school; to fit in or be popular; peer pressures of all sorts; conflicts at home; serious personal or family problems; etc.) Ask the kids to list each source of stress as it is mentioned.

When kids feel they have generated a pretty complete list, ask them to read over their lists individually and check the items that stress them. Have them guess which item got the most "votes," then see if they guessed right.

3 Stress Is Nothing New

It seems like just about everyone here feels stress at some time. Maybe you even discovered that the biggest stresses in your life are the biggies in someone else's life too.

Stress is a common part of life today. But it's nothing new. Way back in Bible times, people faced some pretty stressful things too.

Divide into teams and assign each team one of the following sets of verses. Ask them to read the verses, jot down the stressful events in the person's life, and be ready to report their findings to the other teams.

•*DAVID*

I Samuel 17:4-11, 38-40, 48-50 (David fights an armed bully with only a slingshot—and faith in God.)

I Samuel 17:28-29 (David's brother gets mad at David and calls him arrogant.)

I Samuel 18:6-11 (Saul is so jealous of David that he tries to kill him.)

•*PAUL*

Acts 9:23-25 (Enemies plan to kill Saul [Paul], so he must flee the city.)

Acts 16:22-24 (Paul is beaten and thrown in prison.)

Acts 27:27-44 (Paul is shipwrecked.)

II Corinthians 12:7-10 (Paul suffers from an unnamed physical problem.)

II Timothy 4:10, 14, 16 (Paul is deserted by his friends.)

•*JESUS*

John 11:14-37 (Jesus' good friend Lazarus has died, and Jesus returns to the town where people want Him dead.)

Mark 15:16-20 (Jesus is mocked.)

Matthew 26:14-16, 36-45, 56, 69-75 (Jesus' closest friends desert Him.)

Matthew 27:46 (Even Jesus' Heavenly Father abandoned Him.)

When the teams have given their reports, ask: **Could you identify with any of the stresses these people faced?** (Some don't seem real to us—like killing giants or running from kings. But some are just like ours—brothers picking on us or death of family and close friends, or friends who let us down.)

How would you answer somebody who says that people who love God shouldn't ever feel stressed out? (Countless stories in the Bible demonstrate that Christians aren't any more free than other people from stressful situations. In fact, sometimes being faithful to God puts more stress on you—as you try to resist negative peer pressure, for instance. But it is true that being a Christian gives you resources that other people don't have for coping with stress.)

4 God's Prescription for Coping

The three people we've just read about can tell us something about God's prescription for coping with stress.

1. Remember who's in charge. Read Matthew 6:25-33 and ask kids for other examples of how God takes care of us.

2. Take it one day at a time. Read Matthew 6:34 and ask for practical ways to live out the verse. Supplement with these ideas:

- **Break whatever is causing you stress into manageable pieces.** (If exams are stressing you out, focus first on one class, then on reading through the notes for that class, etc.)
- **Get help.** (Ask a teacher or classmate to help you with an assignment you

can't handle. Talk to your pastor or school counselor if you're facing a major personal or family problem.) Demonstrate this concept by asking a pair of kids to stretch their rubber band as far as they can again. Then have another pair link two rubber bands together and show how much farther they can stretch.

• **Know your limits.** (Don't try to do more than you can handle, even if it is fun stuff. When you are overcommitted, you feel stressed out.) Illustrate this idea by stretching a rubber band until it breaks.

3. **Count on God for help and peace of mind.** Read an example of this from each of the people studied earlier: Psalm 42:11 (David); Philippians 4:6, 7 (Paul); Matthew 26:39 (Jesus). Ask kids to share times when they felt God's peace and comfort in their lives, even if maybe the stressful circumstances did not change.

5 Band Together

Divide into teams. Assign each team one of the top stresses from the list you made in Step 2. Give the teams a few minutes to discuss how to apply God's prescription for coping to this stress, then have them share with the whole group. Invite others to add ideas.

In closing, make a rubber band "sculpture" by linking all the rubber bands together. Because rubber bands are limp, the sculpture will work only if everyone helps hold it up.

Emphasize the importance of holding each other up in stressful times. Brainstorm ways to encourage those facing stress. (Be there for them as a friend; send an encouraging note; offer specific help if it's an area you can help in, such as studying together; refer them to others who can help; pray for them; etc.)

Optional Extras

1. *Psalm Writing.* Write psalms or prayers expressing anxieties and concluding with assurance that God will hear. Share these as closing prayers.

2. *Rubber Band Olympics.* Play several games using the rubber bands; for example: the farthest shot, the most accurate shot, or the most rubber bands shot in a minute, etc.

3. *Support Groups.* Find or form support groups for those dealing with serious problems such as alcoholism, parents' divorce, eating disorders.

DATE USED

How to Say What You Really Feel

BIG IDEA

When we speak the truth in love, we can express our own feelings without putting blame on the other person.

BIBLE INPUT

Ephesians 4:15, 16

BRING:

Bibles
Pencils
Paper

1 Impromptu Skits

Ask for two volunteers to stand in front of the group. For the moment, don't let on that they're going to be participating in an impromptu skit.

Explain to the rest of the group and say: **Choose one of these situations: proposing marriage, asking someone out for the first time; or going out on that first date.** You may want to add other situations to this list. Get kids to yell out their choices, select the first one you hear, and announce it to the actors.

Next, have the kids choose one of these acting styles: slow-motion, aliens from space, Shakespearean, or operatic. Again, have kids yell out the styles and choose the first one you hear.

Finally, choose one of these settings: a roller coaster, a school cafeteria, underwater, an echo chamber, or the dentist's chair.

Turn to your volunteers and say: **By the way, did I mention that this was a skit?** Do give your actors a chance to think on their feet and then let them act out the situation as wild and wacky as they want. After about two minutes, call time and ask for another set of volunteers. Repeat the same selection process. If your kids are enjoying themselves, do another round of skits.

Lead into the session's topic with questions like these:

Was it hard for some of you to let yourself go and express your emotions? Why or why not? (It was a silly situation; you felt embarrassed expressing the emotions in this setting; when everyone's watching you, it's hard to stay serious and concentrate. Others might say that because of the silly situation, they weren't about to express themselves.)

How many of you have ever felt awkward when you wanted to tell someone, "I love you," or express some other emotion in real life?

2 Share Your Tongue-tied Times

Hand out blank paper and pencils to your group. **Some people feel self-conscious saying nice things; others have a hard time expressing their anger or their hurt. As I read this list, write down a key word from each sentence to show which item of the pair is harder for you. For example, if it's harder for you to express hatred than love, write down the word "hatred." When you've finished writing, hold up your paper so everyone else can see it.** After each statement, ask a few kids to explain their choices.

Is it harder to . . .

- **express love or hatred?**
- **say what you really feel to someone you like or to someone you don't like?**
- **say what you really feel to a family member or to a friend?**
- **compliment or criticize?**

3 Speak the Truth in Love

Read Ephesians 4:15. Discuss what it means to "speak the truth in love":

When might it be better to speak the truth about how you feel, even if it would be easier to keep it to yourself? (It's better to tell a parent you love him or her, even if you feel embarrassed; sometimes it is better to express your anger instead of letting it build inside; you might need to confront someone about something he or she doing that is harmful or wrong, even though you are afraid the person will get mad at you.)

Give some examples of how you could speak the truth, but not in love. (It might be true that you're angry, but you could be unloving by lashing out at the person; you might truly be hurt, so you try to hurt the person back.)

Why is it important to express a difficult emotion, like anger, in love? (If you aren't loving, you won't improve the situation; people will be more likely to listen if you are speaking out of love; hard emotions can destroy a relationship if they aren't accompanied by love.)

How do you feel when someone tells you that something you do really bugs him? (Defensive; embarrassed; want to change; feel like it's his problem; want to avoid him.)

Let's learn a way to express some of our hard emotions without putting the other person on the defensive. Hand out paper and pencils and ask kids to write down this sentence, including the blanks:

I feel ____________ when you ____________ .

Give some examples of how to use this sentence:

- To a friend: **I feel left out when you and our other friends don't wait for me at lunchtime.**
- To a parent: **I feel as if you don't trust my judgment when you criticize my friends.**
- To a sibling: **I feel angry when you use my things without asking.**

Explain: **When you say, "I feel angry," instead of, "You make me so mad," you take responsibility for your own emotions instead of putting the blame on the other person. When you say, "when you use my things," instead of "because you always take my stuff," you let the person know the situation that bothers you without accusing him or her of being such a terrible person.**

4 Express Your Uneasy Emotions

Ask each person to write, on separate sheets of paper, two or three situations in which it would be hard to say what one really feels. Have them describe the situations and identify the other persons involved.

Fold the papers in half, mix them up, and have kids take turns drawing one from the pile and roleplaying how they might respond, using the sentence they learned in Step 3. For example, a parent might be overprotective, and it's frustrating for a seventeen year old to be treated like a baby. The response could be something like this: "Mom, I know you love me, but sometimes I feel frustrated when you treat me like a baby."

Or someone might feel used by a friend who gets chummy-chummy whenever he or she needs something. The roleplay response could be like this: "Kendra, I want to be your friend, but I feel used when the only time you call me is when you want something from me."

Encourage them: **Don't worry if you feel awkward or a little unnatural the first few times you try this. Sometimes just stopping to think about how to say what you feel can help you solve a problem instead of making it worse.**

5 Point Out the Positive

Read Ephesians 4:16. **Speaking the truth in love doesn't just mean expressing our difficult feelings. It also means building each other up by focusing on the positives.**

Practice pointing out the positives by inviting volunteers to share something they like about each group member. (If affirmation does not come spontaneously to your group, draw names and give the kids a few minutes to "interview" others on the positive qualities of the person they are assigned. Then have them "report" to the person in front of the whole group.)

Ask: **Is there someone you need to say something positive to this week?** Have kids write down the name of that person and what they want to tell him or her. Encourage them to make time this week to say the positive things they really feel.

Optional Extras

1. *Group Gripes*. Provide an open forum to share feelings about the group. Encourage each person to include at least one positive comment. Allow kids to share frustrations about the group, but urge them not to air problems with individual group members in this public setting. Guide listeners to accept the speaker's feelings without reacting defensively. Model this acceptance when frustrations about leadership are aired!

2. *Put It on Paper*. Letter writing can be a more comfortable way to begin to resolve an ongoing conflict. Invite group members to write a letter expressing feelings, then share it with another person to see if it is indeed truthful and loving.

DATE USED

How to Pray

BIG IDEA

Following a simple pattern of prayer can help us focus on God and others, as well as on our own needs.

BIBLE INPUT

Psalm 34:1-3; 66:18, 19
Hebrews 13:15
I John 1:9
Philippians 4:6
I Thessalonians 5:16-18
I Timothy 2:1

BRING:

Bibles
Pencils
Paper
Package of balloons

1 Put Your Knees to Work

Have teams compete to pass a balloon down the line, held only between the players' knees.

Introduce the topic of prayer: **Many people were taught to pray on their knees when they were children. What are some other positions, actions, or phrases we associate with prayer?** (Folded hands; closed eyes; "thee" and "thou"; bowed head; tacking on the words "in Jesus' name.")

Do you think these are the keys to effective prayer? (Many of them are good things to do, but they do not by themselves make our prayers effective.)

2 Examine ACTS of Prayer

Give teams these sets of verses to read and summarize for the group:

- Psalm 34:1-3; Hebrews 13:15
- Psalm 66:18, 19; I John 1:9
- Philippians 4:6; I Thessalonians 5:16-18
- I Timothy 2:1

After the teams have reported, suggest using the guidelines in these verses as a structure for prayer. If you have kids who have encountered the acronym ACTS before, help them recognize that these passages form the biblical basis for it. Explain the acronym for those who have not heard of it and to refresh the memories of those who have:

Adoration: praising God for who He is

Confession: admitting your sins and asking for forgiveness

Thanksgiving: thanking God for specific things He has done

Supplication: praying for the specific needs of others and yourself

Together come up with examples for each part of the prayer. Use this time to share real prayer requests and praises.

How can this outline for prayer help us as we pray? (Reminds us to keep a balance between praise and requests; prevents us from praying selfish prayers; teaches us directly from the Bible; gives us a focus to keep our minds from wandering when we pray.)

Do you think your prayers will be more effective if you use this outline? (Our prayers will be more pleasing to God when we remember to praise and thank Him and to pray for others. He will be pleased when we try to apply what the Bible teaches us to our praying. In that way our prayers will be more effective. But using ACTS as an outline for prayer doesn't guarantee that we will get what we want, any more than doing the things we talked about in Step 1 will guarantee results. Prayer is meant to be communication with God, not a means of manipulating Him into giving us what we want.)

3 Make It Stick

Divide into small teams and give each team a balloon. Give them three minutes to get their balloon higher than any other team's balloon. They can do whatever they want using whatever resources they can find—except for tape (some kids may try static electricity to stick the balloon to the hair of a team member they've lifted up), but the balloon must stay up for thirty seconds without anyone holding it.

Sometimes we look at our prayers as if they were balloons. We figure that it's up to us to get them high enough for God to take notice. We figure if we pray just right, or live good enough lives, then our prayers will really stick.

4 Offer a Balloon Bouquet

When you compare your prayers to the ACTS outline, do you feel like sometimes you are pretty selfish in what you pray for? Do you ever wonder if God has better things to do than listen to your little needs, or if He gets tired of hearing you ask for the same thing over and over? Do you ever worry that your prayers aren't good enough to get any farther than the ceiling?

Ask a volunter to read Psalm 50:14, 15.

What do you think a "sacrifice of thanksgiving" is? (This psalm refers to prayers of thanks as offerings, much as the Old Testament believers offered animal sacrifices.)

Ask a volunter to read Psalm 116:12, 13.

How does the writer of this psalm say he will try to repay God for all His goodness? (By calling on God's name; that is, praying.)

Ask a volunteer to read I Thessalonians 5:16-18.

What is God's will for you, according to these verses? (To rejoice, pray constantly, and give thanks.)

Point out that the Bible makes it clear that God desires our prayers and receives them with joy, as if they were gifts or offerings. Our prayers can be effective, not because we are so good at praying, but because God wants to hear them and to answer them.

Let's offer some prayers to God as gifts. Give each group member four balloons and some paper and pencils. Invite kids to tear off four or more strips of paper and write a part of a prayer on each one, following the acronym ACTS. When they have written their prayers, have them blow up the balloons and put a strip of paper in each one. If you have markers, let them label the balloons A, C, T, and S.

Close in a group prayer, encouraging kids to hold their balloon bouquets up as a symbolic gesture of offering their prayers to God.

Optional Extras

1. *Prayer Collage*. Provide sheets of newsprint, butcher paper, or poster board. Have kids write four headings (Adoration, Confession, Thanksgiving, and Supplication) and illustrate each one with pictures cut from magazines, their own artwork, and graffiti.

2. *Prayer Support*. As a group, agree on particular people or ministries you will support with regular prayer, both as a group and individually. Pray for them each time your group gets together.

3. *Prayer in Action*. Often God answers prayer through people. Choose a service project that will help you be God's agents in one of the concerns mentioned for supplication in Step 2.

4. *Balloon Games*. Have kids line up and give each of them a balloon. When you say "go," kids should blow up their balloons and then let them go. Measure whose balloon goes the farthest. Or divide kids into teams and see which team can stick the most balloons to the wall or ceiling in three minutes—using only static electricity. Or pair up kids and give each pair a balloon. Partners should kick a balloon to the far end of the room and back, alternating kicks. If the balloon touches the floor, they must start over. The first pair to successfully complete the relay is the winner.

DATE USED

How to Tell a Friend about Jesus

BIG IDEA

Don't think of telling others about Jesus as a "hard sell," but rather as introducing one friend to another.

BIBLE INPUT

Romans 3:10, 23; 5:12; 6:23; 5:8; 10:9, 10

BRING:

Bibles
Pencils
Paper
Dice to roll

1 Describe a Friend

Hand out paper and pencils and ask each person to write his or her name on a piece of paper. Collect, shuffle, and redistribute the papers, making sure no one gets his or her own name.

Have kids describe the person whose name they have by listing personal qualities (such as kindness, musical or athletic ability, etc.) and actions (plays soccer, always says hello to new people, etc.); and to do so in five words. Also, instruct them not to refer to appearance.

When everyone has completed a description, collect them and read them aloud. Make a competition of guessing who is being described. Have each person write down a guess, then award ten points to the writer for every person who correctly identifies his or her description.

Was it easy or hard for you to figure out who was being described? (In many cases it may have been difficult because we so often focus on externals rather than personal characteristics. Or it may have been hard if the writer did not know the person well enough to describe him or her adequately using so few words.)

Was it easy or hard to write a good description? (Probably depended on how well the writer knew the person.)

Would it be easy or hard for you to describe Jesus to someone who didn't know Him? (The better you know Jesus, the easier it is to know what to say about Him. It might be hard to describe Him convincingly because in some ways He is different from anyone else we know.) Have kids try to describe Jesus in five words.

2 Describe Your Friend Jesus

Ask volunteers to name some good friends. Then ask:

- **How and when did you first meet this friend?**
- **What do you like about him or her?**
- **What good things does he or she bring to your friendship? To your life?**
- **Why might others want to get to know your friend?**

Explain that, just as we naturally talk about our good friends and want our new friends to meet our old friends, so we can introduce friends to our friend Jesus. Ask volunteers to answer the same questions about Jesus that you asked about other friends:

- **How and when did you meet Jesus?**
- **What do you like about Him?**
- **What good things does He bring to your friendship? To your life?**
- **Why might others want to get to know Jesus?**

3 Follow the Romans Road

Admit: **Even when we are close to Jesus and want to tell our other friends about Him, it can be hard to know what to say. And it's important to let others know what the Bible says about Jesus, not just to talk about our own experience with Him. Let's look at a good way to do this.**

Distribute paper and assign different group members to write one of the following (the reference only, not the whole verse) in large letters on a single sheet of paper:

- Romans 3:10
- Romans 3:23
- Romans 5:12
- Romans 6:23
- Romans 5:8
- Romans 10:9, 10

If you have more than six kids, have them write any or all of the following, repeating any except START and FINISH so that everyone has something to write:

- START
- FINISH
- Go back 2
- Go forward 2
- Go to next verse

Help your group lay out a room-sized board game using the papers as squares of the board. Make sure the verse squares go in the order listed, and put at least seven sheets of paper (they can be blank or from the second list) between the verse squares.

Divide into teams and have each team choose one player to serve as a human game token. Line the tokens up at the START square and play by these rules:

1. Each team gets one roll of the dice per turn.
2. The game token moves the number of squares indicated by the dice, EXCEPT that he or she must pause on the next verse square.
3. When the token pauses on a verse square, a team member must read the verse aloud. If any member of the team can explain what the verse means, the token finishes out the number of moves on the dice. If no one can explain the verse, the token stays on the square until the next turn.

When the game is over, briefly review the plan of salvation as outlined in the verses. Suggest that kids use the "Romans Road" as a way to tell others about Jesus.

4 Mark Road Signs

Encourage kids that they don't have to memorize the Romans Road to use it in sharing Jesus. If they have their own Bibles with them, instruct kids to mark their Bibles as follows. If they don't have their own Bibles along, urge them to jot down these instructions and mark their Bibles at home.

1. In the front cover of your Bible, write, "Romans 3:10."
2. At Romans 3:10, write, "Romans 3:23."
3. At Romans 3:23, write, "Romans 5:12."
4. At Romans 5:12, write, "Romans 6:23."
5. At Romans 6:23, write, "Romans 5:8."
6. At Romans 5:8, write, "Romans 10:9, 10."

Explain that they can use these "road signs" to guide someone through the plan of salvation. They can read each verse, explain it to the person, then move to the next verse marked.

5 Practice Giving Directions

In pairs, have kids take turns leading each other along the Romans Road. Encourage them to not only find the verses, but they should also explain what they mean in everyday language. Circulate to help and encourage.

Challenge kids to think of someone they need to tell about Jesus. Ask them to think about what first step they could take. Pray for an opening to talk about Jesus? Tell the person about their friendship with Jesus? Share what the Bible says through the Romans Road?

Close with a prayer that kids will be motivated and bold and that the Holy Spirit will open the hearts of their friends.

Optional Extras

1. *Personal Testimony*. As motivation for your group, invite a group member or an outside guest to share how a friend introduced him to Christ.

2. *Friends Night*. Plan a group activity to which kids can bring unsaved friends.

3. *Tracts*. Find tracts that are appropriate for your kids to use and make them available. Talk through the tracts so that kids know how to explain the contents. Or make your own tracts as a group, perhaps using the Romans Road, and photocopy them for kids to use.

DATE USED

How to Find What You're Looking For in the Bible

BIG IDEA

The Bible provides answer for real-life questions and meets real-life needs. Using resources and reading the Bible regularly can help you find what you need, when you need it.

BIBLE INPUT

Psalm 119:9-16

BRING:

Bibles
Pencils
Paper
Concordance

1 An Indoor Scavenger Hunt

Divide into teams and give each team a sheet of paper and a pencil. Instruct teams to list fifteen things that can be found in the room, giving each item's description or function only, not its name. (For example: something red; something used for fastening things; two things whose names rhyme.) Trade lists and see which team can gather all the items first.

2 List Things to Find in the Bible

Part of the challenge of the scavenger hunt was that you weren't always sure just what you were looking for. Sometimes the same is true when we are looking for something in the Bible. If I asked you to find John 3:16, you could probably do it—you would know what you were looking for. But if I asked you to find a passage that talks about how to use your money, it would be a little harder to know where to start.

The Bible has a lot of valuable and helpful things to tell us. Let's brainstorm some of the kinds of things we might want to find in the Bible.

Together, brainstorm things kids might want to find in the Bible (a verse or passage that would encourage them to stick tough times out, a particular promise, a particular story about a Bible character, teaching about the Holy Spirit, etc.) Ask a volunteer to list each suggestion as it is mentioned. When you have generated a good list, work together to group the items into categories (characters, commands, promises, prophecy, etc.) and list each entry alphabetically within its category. Ask each group member to write out the alphabetized list, or at least those items he or she is most interested in.

3 Make a Reference Guide

Using a concordance and any other aids you have, let kids work in pairs to look up passages and write down references beside the items on their lists.

Point out the list of books in the front of the Bible and show kids how to use the page numbers to find the books they don't know well. Demonstrate how to use a concordance by looking up a key word in a passage and checking all the references listed. Provide these additional hints:

- If Jesus said it, it's probably in the Gospels (Matthew, Mark, Luke, John).
- If it's straight instruction, look first in the Epistles. (Point out the Epistles in the list of books at the front of the Bible.)
- If it's a parable, try the Gospels.

- If it's about the early church, look in the Book of Acts.
- If it happened before Jesus was born, look in the Old Testament.
- If it's poetry, start with Psalms.

4 Compete to Find the Passage

Divide into teams and have each team write ten quiz bowl questions/assignments (and answers). For example: Find a passage to read when you're afraid—Psalm 23 or Isaiah 41:10 would be two acceptable answers. Find instructions about sex—Exodus 20:14 or I Corinthians 6:18 are two of many possible answers. Find a passage that would be good to read at a funeral—John 14:1-4 or I Corinthians 15:51-57 would be acceptable.

Let the teams quiz each other, using the guides they wrote in Step 3 to help them. Award 100 points to the person who finds a passage first, and keep track of how much time a team takes to find all ten passages. Declare an individual high scorer and a winning team.

5 Make Everyone a Winner

Acknowledge that some people had an advantage in the competition: those who have been Christians longer are likely to be more familiar with the Bible, and know where to find some things without using a concordance or reference guide.

Read Psalm 119:9-16.

According to these verses, what are some of the benefits that come from knowing God's Word, the Bible? (Young people will be able to live purely; we can avoid sin; we can rejoice as if we were really rich.)

What do we have to do to get these benefits, according to this passage? (Apply what we read to how we live; seek God with a whole heart; "hide" God's Word in our hearts; learn what God teaches; meditate on God's Word; don't neglect God's Word.)

What are some practical ways to do these things? (Don't neglect the Bible; instead, read it regularly on your own; learn what God teaches by paying attention in church, youth group, Sunday School; think about what you read and hear, and try to apply it to your everyday life.)

Point out: **The more time and attention you give to reading and learning from God's Word, the Bible, the more benefit you will get from it. It won't matter whether or not you can win a contest for looking up a passage the fastest; in the ways that really count, you will already be a winner!**

Optional Extras

1. *Treasure Hunt.* Set up a treasure hunt for your opening activity. The hidden treasure could be a Snickers bar, a book, or even five dollars. Explain that the Bible is full of valuable treasure, and this session will provide clues to help them find it.

2. *Resources.* Gather as many resources as you can for use in Steps 3 and 4. If possible, provide several concordances (many Bibles have small concordances in the back), a chain reference Bible, study Bibles, a Bible dictionary, etc. Look for Bibles that have a listing of passages by topic or need ("When you need encouragement, read . . ."). Most of the Bibles placed by Gideons include this feature.

3. *Personal Bible Reading.* Urge kids to make a realistic commitment to personal Bible reading for the next week. Provide suggestions of appropriate passages to get them started, or introduce them to some good youth devotional books.

4. *Follow-up Studies.* Build on what you learned from Psalm 119:9-16 in Step 5 by using Skill Builders 13 (Figuring Out What the Bible Means), 14 (How to Apply the Bible to Your Own Life), and 15 (How to Memorize Bible Verses) to help kids learn God's decrees (Psalm 119:12), live according to His Word (vs. 9), and hide it in their hearts (vs. 11).

DATE USED

Figuring Out What the Bible Means

BIG IDEA

As you read the Bible, ask yourself: What does it say? What does it mean? What does it mean to me? Then rely on the Holy Spirit to help you understand.

BIBLE INPUT

Psalm 19:10
Psalm 119:105
I Corinthians 2:12-16

BRING:

Bibles
Pencils
Paper

1 Make and Break a Code

Divide into teams and give each team a paper and pencils. Assign one of the following verses to each team and make sure they keep it secret. (If you use more than two teams, you can repeat the assignments. Just make sure that, when it is time to decode, no team gets the same passage it encoded.)

- Psalm 19:10
- Psalm 119:105

Instruct the teams to write out their verse and its reference in code for the other team to decipher. They may devise whatever kind of code they wish, as long as it is consistent (the letter *A* is always the same character, for instance) and has some kind of logic to it. Some possibilities:

- Write out the alphabet. Then rewrite it, but start the letter *A* under the letter *F* (or wherever) and continue so that each letter matches up with a different letter. Plug in the new, code letters to write out your verse.
- Use numbers instead of letters.
- Illustrate your verse instead of using words. Or use a combination.

When the teams have written their verses in code, have them exchange and try to break each other's codes.

Did your team find it easy or hard to break the code?

Did you use any special techniques for making it easier? (Some teams may have caught on that they could decipher the reference and then just look up the verse.)

Do you think it would have been harder or easier to break the code by yourself, instead of with a team?

Do some passages in the Bible ever seem to be written in code? What can make the Bible difficult to understand? (Unfamiliar or out-of-date words like "thee" and "doest"; strange situations; events taking place in a time and location we don't know much about.)

Just as teamwork and some good techniques helped you break the codes earlier, we can work together to decipher what the Bible is telling us.

2 Ask: What Does It Say?

The first step in reading the Bible is a pretty obvious one. Just ask yourself: "What does this passage say?" To answer this question, look for key words and also answer the who, what, where, when, and why questions. For example, who wrote the verse and who was it written to?

Ask someone from the team that deciphered Psalm 119:105 to read it aloud.

Without trying to get deep or make any interpretations, what does this verse literally say? (Your Word is a lamp to my feet and a light to my path.)

3 Ask: What Does It Mean?

Next, ask yourself: "What does this verse mean?" This is the time to start looking at context, thinking about metaphors or examples, and remembering other things God teaches in the Bible.

First, let's look at the context. What is meant by "Your Word"? (The Bible; God's teachings.) **How do you know?** (Verse 89 tells us that it is talking about God's Word; we know that the Bible is called the Word; many surrounding verses talk about God's laws and teachings.)

What does a lamp or light for a path do? (Lets you see where you are going; makes the way visible and clear; keeps you from tripping up.)

What do you think the path stands for? (The way we should live; the direction our lives should take.)

So what does it mean that God's Word is a light for your path? (The Bible makes clear how I should live.)

4 Ask: How Does It Apply to Me?

The Bible is not the kind of book you read just to know what it says. Once you know what it says, you have to do something about it. So the last question to ask is: "How does it apply to me?"

How might you apply this particular verse to your life? (I should read the Bible more often so I can know how to live; I can find direction from the Bible when I feel unsure of what to do; I don't have to see the Bible as something I don't understand—instead I know it sheds light on my real life.)

5 Start with the Spirit

Now that you know the three questions to ask, see if you can use them to find out the very first step to understanding what the Bible says.

Ask pairs to read I Corinthians 2:12-16 and work together to understand the passage. After the pairs have spent some time studying the passage, discuss:

According to this passage, what do you think is an essential for understanding what the Bible says? (Being taught by the Spirit; having the "mind of Christ.")

How can we have the mind of Christ? (Only by believing in Him and receiving Him into our lives.)

How can we learn from the Spirit when we read the Bible? (Pray for the Spirit to open our minds and hearts and guide us.)

6 Rap It Up

Ask someone from the team that deciphered Psalm 19:15 to read the verse aloud. Ask another volunteer to say a brief prayer asking for the Spirit to help you all understand. Then divide into three teams, assign each team one of the three questions to ask about Psalm 19:15, and ask them to create and perform a rap, song, or skit illustrating the answer to their question.

- TEAM 1: What does it say? (God's ordinances are more precious than gold and sweeter than honey.)
- TEAM 2: What does it mean? (God's laws and teachings in the Bible are very valuable. They are also satisfying and can give us pleasure.)
- TEAM 3: What does it mean to me? (I shouldn't look at God's guidelines as negative; if I obey God's laws, I'll be happier and more satisfied than if I break them; I want to obey God; I can find pleasure in reading His Word.)

Optional Extras

1. *Bible Translations*. Display a variety of translations and let kids evaluate which are most readable; include the original Hebrew and Greek if you can.

2. *Group Devotions*. Invite group members to lead brief devotions at future meetings following the format of the three questions. Work with them individually to give them confidence in their selections and presentations.

3. *Personal Devotions Guide*. Help your group write a personal devotions guide. Assign each pair a verse or passage and ask them to develop a page for the guide. Try this format:
   - Write out the verse.
   - Write a brief prayer asking for the Holy Spirit's guidance.
   - Write out the three questions with space for writing answers.
   - Pose a challenge that suggests one way to apply the verse this week.

DATE USED

How to Apply the Bible to Your Own Life

BIG IDEA

The Bible is a book of truth, not trivia. So it's important not to just read it, but to live out what it teaches.

BIBLE INPUT

James 1:22-25
James 2:14-17
Matthew 25:31-46

BRING:

Bibles
Pencils
Paper
Trivia game (not one based on Bible knowledge)

1 Pursue Trivia

Play a few rounds of a trivia game (not one based on Bible knowledge), then discuss which pieces of information are useful in everyday life. Beyond winning a game, what good are they? Explain that knowledge for its own sake can be good and satisfying, however the things we learn from the Bible are not in that category.

2 Apply the Truth

Read James 1:22-25 and briefly discuss the difference between merely listening to the Word and doing what it says.

If you read the Bible but don't do what it says, some people might call you forgetful or stupid or a hypocrite. But listen to what God says.

Read James 2:14-17.

What is the consequence of not living out your faith, not applying the truth? (Your faith is as good as dead, and there's no evidence you are saved.)

If you need any more convincing, listen to this. Read Matthew 25:31-46.

Remind your students that we are all saved by grace through faith, not by the good things we do. But point out that if we do not put our faith into action, it probably isn't true faith; it is probably dead.

3 Stand by the Truth

Distribute paper and pencils and ask kids to write out the following phrases, one to a page:

- A promise I can claim
- A command I should obey
- A good example for me to follow
- A bad example for me to avoid
- A sin in my life I need to confess
- A feeling or situation I identify with
- A new thought about God

Place the pages in various parts of the room.

Assign each person one of the passages you looked at in Step 2 (James 1:22-25; James 2:14-17; Matthew 25:31-46). Give them a few minutes to reread the passage silently and find something in it that matches one of the phrases placed around the room.

When everyone has had a chance to think, ask them to go and stand by the sign that represents something they found in their passage. Assure them that each passage has several points of application, so there is no one "right" answer. Ask several volunteers to share why they chose the sign they did, then have kids reread their passages and see if there is another point of application they can make.

Some examples of applications:

- A promise I can claim: If I obey God's commands, I will be blessed (James 1:25).
- A command I should obey: Don't just listen to God's Word, do it (James 1:22).
- A good example for me to follow: Caring for the poor (Matthew 25:34-40).
- A bad example for me to avoid: Wishing people well but not doing anything to help them (James 2:16).
- A sin in my life I need to confess: Ignoring the needs of others (Matthew 25:45).
- A feeling or situation I identify with: I don't always see how helping others is the same as doing it to Jesus (Matthew 25:45).
- A new thought about God: I don't usually think of God being so angry with people over good things they didn't do (Matthew 25:41); usually I think of sin as the bad things you do.

4 Pursue Truth, Not Trivia

Have kids replace the trivia questions in the trivia game with "truth" questions. Have them tear paper in the size of the game cards, then write a Scripture reference on each card. Ask each person to make three to five cards, using any Bible passages he or she wishes. If you really want to get fancy, have them designate a category on the back of the card, based on the types of application listed in Step 3.

Here are a couple of examples of passages and categories, with possible applications in parentheses.

- Mark 9:33-35/A feeling or situation I identify with (Like the disciples, I want to be first; I want to be the greatest at the expense of others.)
- Ephesians 4:29-32/A command I should obey or a sin in my life I need to confess (I should build up others by what I say, not grieve the Holy Spirit, get rid of bitterness, rage, anger, and be kind and compassionate. Or I need to confess my sin of bitterness, anger, and so on.)

Collect and shuffle the cards, then divide the kids into teams and play a few rounds of the trivia game, this time asking teams to name an application for the passage listed. If kids designated categories, use those categories instead of the categories on the trivia game.

Conclude by affirming the importance of what your group has learned. Remind them that truth is more important than trivia. But also remind them that knowing how to apply the Bible is only the first part of living out your faith; the second part is actually doing it!

Optional Extras

1. ◆ *Mirror.* Illustrate James 1:23, 24 by giving volunteers hand mirrors and allowing themselves thirty seconds to study their faces. Then take away the mirrors, apply shaving cream to their faces, and have them try to "shave" with straight razors (without blades!). Or have male volunteers try to apply lipstick without looking at themselves in the mirror.

2. ◆ *Group Application.* Decide on a practical way your group could apply what you've learned from Matthew 25:31-46 (organize a food and clothing drive; volunteer in a soup kitchen; sponsor a needy child; etc.). Or choose a different passage for your group application. Try Ephesians 4:29-32 (relationships within the group) or Psalm 100 (worship).

3. ◆ *Application Forms.* Together draw up a form to use after each youth group meeting, Sunday School class, or sermon helping kids spell out specific applications. Put the phrases from Step 3 into question form to guide kids in thinking through what they have learned. Maybe you can even use the form to review the relevance of your lessons!

DATE USED

How to Memorize Bible Verses

BIG IDEA

You probably have a better memory than you realize. A few techniques can help you memorize Bible verses easily.

BIBLE INPUT

Joshua 1:8
Proverbs 3:6

BRING:

Bibles
Pencils
Paper

1 Jog Your Memory with Jingles

Divide into teams. Give each team paper and pencils and have them make a "Complete the Jingle" quiz. They should write out the first parts of ten commercial slogans that they think the other team will be familiar with, leaving each jingle unfinished. (For instance: "Get Met . . ." [It Pays].) They can also use jingles for TV shows and movies. ("Here's the story—of a lovely lady—who was bringing up three very lovely girls. . . .")

Tell teams that their goal is not to stump the other team, but to come up with the most jingles that the other team can complete. Let them choose whether to give a written quiz or to give it orally, singing or saying the first part of the jingle and letting the other team complete it.

2 Map Out a Method

Point out to kids that the quizzes they just took show that they have pretty powerful memories. Ask: **What are some of the reasons that you are able to memorize those jingles so well?** As kids respond, emphasize the following:

- Music: in many cases the tune sticks in your head
- Repetition: you hear the jingles over and over
- Association: you picture a product or a show with the jingle
- Hearing: you don't just read them, you hear them
- Place: you're in the same place—in front of the TV—when you hear many of the jingles

Explain: **We can use the same things that make silly commercial jingles stick in our memories; only we can use them to make it easier to memorize something really worthwhile—God's Word.**

But why memorize God's Word? Get kids to suggest some of their reasons, and then call on a volunteer to look up Joshua 1:8 and read it aloud.

Note: The following two questions are from Skill Builder 13, "Figuring Out What the Bible Means."

- **What is this verse saying?** (Joshua wasn't to let the Book of the Law depart from his mouth, but he was to meditate on it day and night so he would be careful to do everything it says. If he did this, then Joshua would prosper and be successful.
- **What does this verse mean?** (If we meditate and memorize God's Word and let it saturate our actions and thinking, we'll prosper and be successful. You might want to clarify that you're talking about God's definition of prosperity and success, not people's.)

I think prosperity and success in God's eyes are pretty good reasons for memorizing Scripture, so let's get started!

Refer to the list above and have kids write down the methods for aiding memorization. Then give an example of how each could help you memorize Proverbs 3:6:

"In all your ways acknowledge him, and he will make your paths straight."

• Music: Sing the verse to the tune of "There was a farmer had a dog, and Bingo was his name-o." Instead of singing "B-I-N-G-O," sing "Proverbs 3 verse 6." Point out that you don't have to make up your own songs all the time; some Bible verses are already set to music in hymnals or by Christian recording artists.

• Repetition: Have the group sing the verse to the tune of the silly BINGO song, replacing a word with a clap on each repetition just as you would in BINGO. ("Proverbs 3 verse [clap]," etc.) Your group will have this verse memorized by the end of the last repetition, guaranteed! Explain that repetition doesn't have to involve singing; it might mean reading, reciting, or writing a verse over and over.

• Association: Distribute paper and pencils, and have kids make some kind of visual association for the verse. They could draw a person surfing (in all your "waves"), saying hi to God (acknowledge Him), and heading toward a straight road (and He will make your paths straight). Or they could draw a rebus, replacing some of the words of the verse with pictures (a box of ALL laundry detergent in the place of the word "all," etc.)

• Hearing: Point out that you've already used the sense of hearing by singing the verse. Other ways include reading and reciting the verse aloud, taping it and re-playing it to yourself, listening to a commercial tape with a Scripture song on it.

• Place: Explain that some people learn best if they set a consistent time and place for memorizing. Options include: singing or reciting in the shower; placing the verse where you can read it while you do dishes or some other stationary chore; listening to a tape in the car; etc.

Invite kids to suggest any other methods they've found helpful for memorizing. They have memorized formulas, equations, and dates for school; they can apply those skills to memorizing Scripture. Have them add any new suggestions to the list of methods they wrote down earlier.

3 Pick a Passage to Practice On

Give group members some time to practice the methods of memorizing. Distribute Bibles and let each person choose a verse or passage, or suggest they choose one from these lists:

• FAVORITES
John 3:16
Psalm 23
Psalm 100
Exodus 20:1-17 (the Ten Commandments)
Matthew 22:37-40 (the Great Commandment)
Matthew 6:9-13 (the Lord's Prayer)
Matthew 28:18-20 (the Great Commission)

• VERSES FOR WITNESSING
Romans 3:10

Romans 3:23
Romans 5:12
Romans 6:23
Romans 5:8
Romans 10:9,10
• ENCOURAGEMENT AND ASSURANCE
I Corinthians 10:13
Hebrews 4:15, 16
I John 1:9

Encourage group members to use as many of the methods in Step 3 as they find helpful. Urge them to memorize and review their chosen verses over the week, and consider having people report back next week on how successful they were.

Optional Extras

1. *Memory Games*. Affirm kids' memorizing abilities in one of these ways:

• Invite kids to bring in favorite music tapes. Play songs for them and see how many can sing along. Or do the same with a popular radio station.

• Set up your own "Concentration"-style game where kids compete to find matches in an array of pictures, playing cards, or words. Or use a commercial memory game like "Simon."

• Let your group write a quiz on a favorite topic, if they have one in common (baseball stats, etc.)

• Compete to see who can list the most correct local phone numbers from memory, then call or look them up to confirm that they are correct.

2. *Scripture in Song*. Familiarize group members with the many Bible verses that are already set to music. You might:

• Collect a variety of tapes of contemporary Christian songs that are taken straight from Scripture, and play them during the session.

• Distribute the song books your church uses and have kids find the songs that are straight from Scripture (kids may be surprised at how much Scripture they already know from singing these songs).

3. *Motivation for Memorization*. Assign teams to imagine they are in concentration camps and want to "write" as much of the Bible as they can from the verses they know by heart. Or give them an assignment like one of these: demonstrate from Scripture that Jesus is truly God; lead an unbeliever to Jesus; argue from Scripture for creation in your biology class. NOTE: Don't use this activity with kids who are new in the Word and haven't memorized any verses.

4. *Memory Marathon*. Plan a Bible memory contest for a future meeting, and choose one or more passages for each group member to learn. Announce and award prizes if that's an appropriate motivator for your group.

DATE USED

I'm Really Angry!

BIG IDEA

Controlling your temper doesn't mean never getting mad. It means expressing your anger in an appropriate way.

BIBLE INPUT

Acts 15:36-40
II Timothy 4:9-11
John 2:12-17
James 1:19
Ephesians 4:26

BRING:

Bibles
Pencils
Paper
Plastic trash can

1 Put On an Impromptu Skit

Grab four kids just before your meeting to open the session with a skit. Three kids come in one at a time with a message for Rodney (or Rhonda, if you like). Open the skit by saying: **Rodney is going to get some news. After watching, be ready to tell what you think about how Rodney received the news.**

Turn a trash can upside down for Rodney to use as a seat. As Rodney receives each of the following messages, he responds pleasantly and passively. He smiles and acts pleased to have heard the news.

- Rodney's two-timing girlfriend comes in and says nicely, "I know you don't realize it, but for the last six months that you've been dating me exclusively, I've also been dating your best friend. In fact, some nights I went out with him after you brought me home. I hope you don't mind, but after we go to the prom, let's call it quits, OK?"
- A suspicious friend says angrily, "I don't care how many times you tell me that you tried to call and invite me to your party. I'll never believe you. You just didn't want me to come and you can't convince me any differently."
- A bad-news bearer says excitedly, "Did you hear about Carla? She's a good friend of yours, isn't she? Some girls played a prank over the weekend and Carla got the blame for it. She's been suspended from the cheerleading squad and may lose her scholarship. Those girls know this is happening, but they aren't going to speak up."

Discuss the skit with questions like these:

- **What did you think about Rodney's response?**
- **How would you have responded to news like this?**
- **Which do you think would have been the hardest to take?**
- **What would have been a more natural response than his?**
- **What kinds of emotions would you be feeling?**

Probably the concept of anger will arise. If it doesn't, bring it up yourself. Point out that anger is, at times, the most natural, most appropriate response someone can have. Follow up with questions such as:

- **What kinds of things make you angry?**
- **What is it like to get really angry all at once?**
- **What is it like to be angry for a long time?**

2 Stage a Paper Wad Fight

Distribute paper and pencils and instruct kids to write down things they get mad about, one thing to each page. They are not to sign the paper or identify themselves in any way. They may use up to ten pieces of paper. Then have kids crumple each piece of paper into a ball. Divide into teams for a paper wad fight and have the teams combine their artillery for a good showing. Encourage them to work out their anger in a playful way.

For a great paper wad fight, put two tables on their sides as forts. Place a trash can in the middle. The objective of each team is to nab the trash can without being hit by paper wads. Whichever team winds up with the trash can wins.

When the war is won, gather together all the wads of paper in the trash can and use them for Step 3.

3 Rank Reasons for Rage

Distribute the paper wads among small groups. Have each group keep a record of the reasons their peers become angry, looking for reasons which are the most common. After the small groups have tabulated their responses, come together and combine the rankings.

Discuss any reasons that show up many times. Talk about why and how these things trigger anger. Target for discussion any issues that show up often in your group.

Collect the papers once again in the trash can.

4 Apply Some Rules

Point out three rules for dealing with anger:

1. Talk to the person you are actually angry with.
2. Talk about what you're really angry about.
3. Try to make the relationship better, not get revenge.

Then read the case studies below and ask for suggestions of how each main character could follow these three rules.

A. **Toni was angry. She found out why Amanda didn't talk to her on Saturday. Amanda was going to a party at Will's house and Toni wasn't invited. It wasn't so bad to not be invited. But was that any reason to not talk to somebody? It really wasn't the party. Really! And she wasn't mad at Will for not inviting her. He can invite anyone he wanted. But did Amanda have to be a snob about it?**

B. **Josh is having a hard time deciding who he is angry with. He lives with his mom and Don, who married Josh's mom three months ago. Since Josh's mom and Don got married, they have been away every weekend and Josh's mom doesn't depend on Josh like she used to. On top of it all, sometimes Don talks rough to Josh's mom, and she just lets him! Josh is finding every excuse not to go home at all. When he is at home, he blows up easily and feels miserable.**

C. **Paul and Barnabas got so angry once, the New Testament tells us, that they parted ways, broke up a team.** Review with the group Paul and Barnabas's meeting and their joining with John Mark. Read Acts 15:36-40. Discuss the first two rules of dealing with anger. Before discussing the third read II Timothy 4:9-11. Point out that there had obviously been some healing in the relationships, for Paul was now reconciled with Mark.

D. **Jesus got very angry one day when he came to the temple.** Read John 2:12-17. **Why was Jesus angry? How does His response relate to our three rules?**

Read James 1:19 and Ephesians 4:26. Ask for suggestions of how either of these Scriptures could be relevant to any of the four case studies. Brainstorm specific ways Toni and Josh could deal with their anger.

5 Work Out Differences

Demonstrate the importance of dealing with your anger by taking the angry paper wads out of the trash can and trying to put them all in your pockets, down your shirt, etc.—to carry them with you somehow. **We can get overloaded with our own anger if we never deal with it, but only carry it.**

Sometimes we must confront. Take a paper wad out of your pocket and throw it at someone.

Sometimes we must deal with the anger within ourselves. Take a paper wad, open and read it, then tear it up and put it back in the trash can.

Discuss the following options for dealing with anger when confrontation is impossible:

- Go to someone safe and unrelated to the situation to vent your feelings
- Write a letter (that you never send) to the person with whom you are angry
- Forgive the person, reminding yourself that your own happiness is more important than proving the other person wrong
- If that person has hurt or abused you, make a plan for not allowing him or her the opportunity to do it again.

Close by reading Ephesians 4:26 again. Give kids a few minutes to reflect and pray about any angry feelings they feel ready to deal with in proper ways.

Optional Extras

1. *Safe Release*. Bring some blow-up clowns (the kind that bounce back up when you hit them) to the session and have an anger therapy session. Let the kids hit the balloons and work out their anger.

2. *Professional Opinion*. Invite a counselor or doctor to come in and address anger with the group. Ask him or her to talk about the physical effects of anger.

DATE USED

I'm Just Too Shy

BIG IDEA

There's nothing wrong with being quiet or enjoying being alone, but if we start hiding from life, we need to stop and make sure we aren't letting fears box us in.

BIBLE INPUT

I Samuel 10:17-24
Exodus 3:10—4:13
II Timothy 1:7

BRING:

Bibles
Pencils
Paper
A large dictionary

1 Act the Part

As kids arrive, write on their right palms "S" or "NS." The "S" people must act shy. The "NS" people must act not shy. As they are acting, they must guess what is written in each other's palm. When someone's palm is diagnosed correctly, he or she must hold that hand in the air, but keep guessing and acting the part until the status of everyone's palm has been revealed. Debrief with questions such as:

- **What were your clues? How did you guess?**
- **Did any of you have to act unnaturally to play your part?**
- **How did it feel for one of you outgoing people to act shy?**
- **How about the opposite?**

2 Define Shyness

Have someone look up and read the definition of shyness in a large dictionary.

As a group, make a list of traits or behaviors that are associated with shyness. Then put together a group definition of what it means to be shy. Discuss these questions:

- **Can the same person be shy sometimes and sometimes not?**
- **Is there anyone here who has never felt shy?** Make the point that most people have felt shy at some time or the other.
- **What makes us shy sometimes?**
- **What are some good things about being shy?** (Shy people can have a calming, quieting influence on a noisy group; shy people can find pleasure in doing things alone that others might miss.)
- **What are some things about being shy that you don't enjoy?** (Feeling uncomfortable around others; worrying about being called on or put on the spot; wanting to make friends but not having the nerve.)
- **What is the difference between someone who just enjoys being alone and someone who is painfully shy?**

Lead the discussion into that of fear. Have someone look up and read the definition of fear in the dictionary.

- **What kind of fears can make us shy?** (Being laughed at or rejected; making a mistake; being embarrassed.)
- **Describe what that kind of fear feels like.**

3 Find Shy People in the Bible

Say something like: **Do you remember who Saul was? Saul was the first king of Israel, chosen by God. For many years he led Israel well. Can you imagine a king being shy? Let's look a one little video clip of Scripture where Saul was probably feeling a little shy.** Either paraphrase or have someone read I Samuel 10:17-24 to the group. Repeat Saul's hiding place several times. **Why do you think Saul was hiding? Why did he feel shy at that moment?**

Next break into groups to read Exodus 3:10—4:13 and list the things that Moses was shy about. (Not important enough [3:11]; they won't believe me [4:1]; I don't speak well [4:10].)

When is being shy, too shy? What is the dividing line between just being a shy person and being a fearful person? Point out that when we are so quiet and reserved that we sit back, wishing we were more involved in what is going on around us, then we are too shy. Some people, however, compensate by talking too much and showing off. The key is to identify our fear and move closer to life.

Have someone read II Timothy 1:7. Point out that God created us as we are. **Some of us are loud and talkative. Some of us are quiet and reserved. But God does not want our lives run by fear. If our shyness is fear, then we should try to overcome it.**

4 Making Up a Line

We can all feel a little shy about meeting people. Explain to the group that a "line" is an introductory statement that allows you to open conversation with someone you don't know. Have fun with group members making up lines with which they can meet people. Start with the classic: "Haven't I seen you somewhere before?" If your group can appreciate it, have some fun with the lines guys and girls use to meet each other. Tease some of your "Casanovas" by asking them to share their best lines.

5 Spell SHY

Give everyone a piece of paper. Assign each one of the letters S, H, or Y. (Do this evenly as if you are counting off by three to divide them into groups.) Form two concentric circles. Have the inside circle walk to the left and the outside circle walk to the right. When you call halt, they must join with two other people to spell "SHY." Then they switch letters with those people and start around the two circles again.

Each time you form into a different group, practice introducing and meeting each other.

You might also want to also try some variations on the theme:

- **All same letters together.**
- **Everyone stand by someone with a different letter.**
- **Every *H* find a Y.**
- **Every *S* find an *H*.**
- **Stand with one other person of your same letter.**

6 *Plan a Strategy*

Conduct a brainstorming session in which you discuss ways to make youth group a safe place where shy people can feel at home. Discuss options such as having greeters at the door and introducing members to guests each session. Name tags are a good option as well. What else will make your group "visitor-friendly?"

Encourage the shy people in your group to take risks and broaden their horizons a little. Encourage your non-shy members to be safe people to help their shy friends break out of the shy mode once in a while.

Close in prayer, asking God to help your kids overcome their fears.

Optional Extras

1. ◆ *Video Opener*. Pull together a group of kids to make a short video on a shy person and an outgoing person. Have them show the two in the same situations, but show how differently they respond. Make it crazy. Make it wild. Show it at the beginning of your meeting.

2. ◆ *Shy Persons Panel*. Invite adults who were shy as youths to come in as a panel on shyness. Line up a few questions of your own to get the group going, then open up the floor for the group to ask questions.

DATE USED

I Don't Have Enough Money

BIG IDEA

If we don't have enough money, then we must either create more income or need less stuff.

BIBLE INPUT

I Timothy 6:10
Luke 16:10-13
Matthew 6:19-21; 25-33

BRING:

Bible
Pencils
Paper
Quarter

1 Play Spenders and Savers

Divide the group equally in half. Indicate a dividing line across the room. Line the teams up along each side of that line, facing each other. Name one team the "Spenders" and one the "Savers."

Toss a coin—heads savers, tails spenders. When you call how the coin fell (savers or spenders), each member of that team must run to the back wall before anyone from the other team tags him or her. Any player that is tagged must join the other team.

Repeat this process until one team has taken over the other.

2 Ask How Much Is Enough

Break into small groups and seat each in a circle. Each person must take a turn stating either, "I don't have enough money," or, "I have enough money," to which the group must ask, "How much is enough?" Then that person must answer how much money would be enough for him or her. ("Enough is enough to buy a car" or "pay for college.")

3 Compare Life-styles to Cars

Bring the groups back together and ask volunteers to state their criteria for enough money. Ask for discussion from the group on the criteria volunteered.

Start a discussion with: **"If someone said, 'He wants a Cadillac life at Volkswagen prices,' what would he mean?"**

Pick cars of different classes that your group can relate to. Assign each car to a kind of life-style. (For instance, Volkswagen, Pontiac, Mercedes, Rolls Royce.) Discuss what level of life-style is associated with each car. Get specific with the kinds of things a person with a Volkswagen life-style would do for fun versus what someone with a Cadillac life-style would do.

Then discuss what life-style your group members want.

- **What determines a person's life-style?**
- **How is your life-style related to material possessions?**
- **How is your life-style related to the kinds of activities you take part in?**
- **If we talk about being at a higher standard of living, what do we mean?**
- **Is it wrong to want to be at a higher standard of living?**
- **Is it more holy to be poor than rich? Is it more holy to be rich than poor?**

4 Ways to Create More Income

State the big idea of the session. Then ask: **If we truly do not have enough money, what are ways we can get more?** Make as long a list as possible of the ways to get money. (Ask for it; be given it; steal; earn; find; sell; trade; borrow; earn a scholarship; inherit; swindle; con; beg; pawn things; etc.)

If you don't have a board or overhead, have the kids copy the list on paper so you can refer back to it as a group. First strike out the ways to get money that are immoral. Then circle the ways that require special knowledge or access that your teens don't feel they have. Finally have them draw arrows to the ways that are possible for them.

5 Need Less Stuff

There is always the possibility that we cannot at this time provide more income for ourselves. There is also the option that we want too much anyway. Either way, we must know how to set priorities with our spending. If we can't buy it all, what can we cut out?

As a group, make a list of five items that would be fun to have, three items that your kids need to have (maybe for school), and one item they would give as a gift at a birthday party. List suggested prices beside each item. Add up the prices at the bottom. Then assign a budget of about 60% of the total.

Break into pairs and have each pair decide how they will prioritize their items. What will they leave out?

When you come back together, discuss not only what they decided but how they arrived at their decisions.

6 Establish a Life-style

Our little spending decisions add up to our life-style. We don't always sit and think, "Now, what do I want my life-style to be." More often it just happens as our habits form. But it is often a good idea to stop and examine the life-style we are establishing. Scripture doesn't tell us how much we should spend on what. But it does provide some guidelines that we can follow.

Divide into groups and assign each group one of the Scripture passages below. Each passage has a suggested key phrase.

Each group should read the Scripture, work through the discussion questions, and prepare to pantomime the key phrase for the whole group. After the large group guesses the idea, each small group should share how this passage applies to their money life-style.

- I Timothy 6:10 (don't love money)
  - -So is money the root of all evil?
  - -What does it mean to love money?
  - -If you love money, how does it affect your life-style?
- Luke 16:10-13 (serve God, not money)
  - -What kind of life-style is a trustworthy one?
  - -How can you show you can be trusted with a little?
  - -If we can't manage a little income, do you think we will be able to handle a big income better?
  - -What does it mean to serve money? To serve God?
  - -If you serve money, what will your life-style be like?
- Matthew 6:19-21 (Store heavenly treasures)
  - -What are earthly treasures?
  - -What are heavenly treasures?
  - -How do we go about storing either?
  - -How does this affect our life-style regarding money?
- Matthew 6:25-33 (seek God's kingdom first)
  - -If we seek God's righteousness, does that mean we'll get everything we want?
  - -If we seek God's kingdom first, what other things are we putting it before?
  - -How would it affect the way we use money if we sought God's kingdom first?

Encourage kids to evaluate their money life-styles in light of God's principles.

Optional Extras

1. *Raising Money*. If your church allows fund-raising, decide on a specific need the youth group has and chart a course for how they can raise the money.

2. *Price Tags*. Bring the following items to this session: a funky outfit, jewelry, an electronic gadget, sack of groceries, college catalog, two videos or movie passes. Write out realistic price tags for each item and place the tag face down. Call the names of several volunteers to "come on down" and guess the prices of the items. Buzz the kids who don't even come close; cheer the kids who come within ten dollars. Talk about some of your kids' spending habits.

DATE USED

I Don't Like My Body

BIG IDEA

Sometimes we think that we can't be happy or attractive unless we have perfect bodies. But God—and most people—don't judge us simply on our figures or physiques.

BIBLE INPUT

II Corinthians 10:12
I Samuel 16:6, 7
Matthew 6:25-27
Romans 12:1-3

BRING:

Bible
Pencils
Paper

1 Make That Shape

Clear the floor and divide into groups. Call out shapes and have the groups form that shape either on the floor or standing. Start easy: triangle, square, circle. Throw in some crazies too: steering wheel, half moon. Include the shapes used to describe body shape: hourglass, pear.

Afterward discuss:

• **Is there any reason one of these shapes is better than another? Is a circle better than a triangle? A square better than an hourglass?**

• **What if I said, I'm making a wheel. Is one shape better than the other?** (Yes, because one rolls and the others don't—very well, anyway. Some shapes are better for certain purposes, but not just of themselves.)

2 Dream Up the Ideal Girl or Guy

Send guys to one side of the room and girls to the other. Have the guys complete the statements in the first column; girls, the statements in the second column. In case of disagreement, majority rules.

• Guys like girls who . . .
a. laugh at their jokes.
b. confront them on important issues.
c. let them win.
d. other ________________.

• Girls like guys who . . .
a. are big and strong
b. are sensitive
c. are in love with them.
d. other ________________.

• The ideal girl is one who . . .
a. has blue eyes, blond hair, and a good figure.
b. has dark hair, brown eyes, and a good figure.
c. likes you back.
d. other ________________.

• The ideal guy is one who . . .
a. has blue eyes, blond hair, and big muscles.
b. has dark hair, brown eyes, and big muscles.
c. listens to your feelings.
d. other ________________.

• How a girl looks is . . .
a. the most important thing.
b. one important thing.
c. not as important as whether she laughs at your jokes.
d. other ________________.

• How a guy looks is . . .
a. the most important thing.
b. one important thing.
c. not as important as whether he listens to your feelings.
d. other ________________.

When the groups have finished, have them predict how the other group answered its questions, and then write each prediction on a separate sheet of paper.

Bring the groups back together and play a version of "The Newlywed Game." Have the girls answer their questions, and compare their answers to what the guys predicted. Do the same with the guys. Award 25 points for each correct prediction.

• **Where do we get our ideas of the ideal man or woman?** (Magazines; media; talking to each other, our parents, our friends.)

• **Why is it hard to like ourselves if we don't fit the ideal stereotype?**

(If your group is all one gender, have them answer their questions and predict what the other gender might say, then discuss areas of disagreement.)

3 Rate Yourself

Distribute paper and pencils. **On a scale of one to ten, with ten being perfection, how would you rate yourself from the neck up? From your neck down?** Give kids a chance to write down their ratings. If your kids would like, they may pair up with someone of the same gender and talk about their ratings. Don't pressure anyone to discuss his or her rating. (Or tally the ratings anonymously.)

4 Suggest Scripture Applications

Let's just suppose that as God was thinking about inspiring the Bible, He had in mind that we would be here on this day trying to figure out how to deal with the things we don't like about ourselves. And let's just suppose that He included some Scriptures particularly to help us in this issue. Let's read some Scriptures and you suggest ways that God may have wanted us to apply these passages to help us accept ourselves. This can be done in small groups or as a large group. Try to get several possible applications from each Scripture.

- Psalm 139:13-16 (God planned us physically)
- II Corinthians 10:12 (comparisons aren't too wise)
- I Samuel 16:6, 7 (outward vs. inward)
- Matthew 6:25-27 (value to God)
- Romans 12:1-3 (we are acceptable offerings)

5 Compare Perception and Reality

• **What are some things about ourselves we can not easily change?** (Height, our laugh, skin color or type, hair type, etc.)

• **What are some things about ourselves we can change?** (Weight, health, cleanliness, hair style.)

• **What can we do to know if we are as bad as we think we are?** (Ask someone you trust.)

Ask the group to quietly think about the next question:

• **Have I come to believe that I am worthless because of something I don't like about myself?** After some silence, remind the group that none of our external traits affects how much God loves us or how much we are worth to Him. **We don't ever have to let our whole sense of worth be defined by one part of our body, or by our body itself.**

Read Romans 8:37-39.

6 Read a Story

Close the session with the story below.

I went to Lisa's funeral yesterday. Lisa was a few years younger than I. She wasn't a model, but she had a great smile and everyone liked her. But Lisa didn't believe anyone liked her. She only concentrated on the things she didn't like about herself and became more and more depressed. No matter what we said to cheer her up, she was down.

One day she shot herself in the head with her dad's gun. I have to admit I'm sort of angry. Everybody has things about themselves they don't like. Why did Lisa have to do something so unfixable?

At the funeral the preacher said, "We grieve the fact that Lisa's mind betrayed her and she couldn't come to see herself as we saw her and as the Lord saw her."

I've thought about that a lot since then. There are a lot of things I don't like about myself. I get so tired of comparing myself to the models in the magazines. But now that Lisa's gone, I sometimes wonder if we need to throw away the magazines and everything else that makes us feel not good enough and just give ourselves a break. And focus on God's love for me and love each other more.

Optional Extras

1. *Good Grooming*. Take an opportunity to discuss grooming. Separate guys and girls and have some adults from the church give a mini-seminar on making the most of your looks. This can be especially effective with junior high/middle school kids, as they try to adjust their grooming and appearance to their rapidly changing bodies.

2. *Balloon Shapes*. Make some sculpture balloons available to your group at the opening of the session. Let them twist the balloons into different shapes as you open your discussion on one shape not being better than another. Then use the balloons as an object lesson of God forming us for His purposes.

DATE USED

I'm Way Too Busy

BIG IDEA

When we are too busy, we don't have time to do anything well. We must learn to decide what things are important to us and say no to the rest.

BIBLE INPUT

Luke 19:10
Mark 1:35
Mark 2:15-17

BRING:

Bible
Pencils
Paper
Alarm clock

Note: Throughout the lesson, time everything. Whether you're passing out paper or organizing into teams—time it. Be very obvious about your time-consciousness.

1 Find Your Best Pace

Give each person a piece of paper and explain the relay this way: **You may fold, crumple, or tear your paper any way you want, as long as you're fairly sure you can balance it on the back of one hand from the starting line to the rest of the members on your relay team.**

Position half of each team at the starting line and the other half about twenty paces away. Again, the objective is to balance the paper on the back of one hand until players get to their next team members. If they drop the paper, they must go back to where they dropped it and start again.

After you've run the relay, hand out more paper and run the race again to see if your kids can improve on their times.

Debrief with questions like these:

• **This race was not only quantitative but qualitative. What does that mean?** (You had to do more than cover a certain distance—or quantity; you also had to meet a certain qualification while you were running—balancing the paper.)

• **Did you have to pace yourself?**

• **How did you work on improving your time the second time you ran the race?**

• **In what kinds of sports activities do you need to pace yourselves?**

• **Do you ever have to pace yourselves in school? How?**

2 Know Your Limits

Divide into small groups and assign each group the two tasks below. Set your alarm clock to go off in seven minutes after you explain the tasks. (You may wish to adjust the time according to how many are in the small groups.)

• TASK 1: Each person in the group must answer this question out loud to the group. **When you are too busy, what is the first thing to go?**

• TASK 2: Each group must come up with five ways to complete this sentence. The more specific and crazier, the better: **You know you're too busy when. . . .**

When the alarm goes off, come back together and have each group read its five statements. Gauge the group's response to judge which standards of too-busy-ness hit home with your kids.

3 Establish Priorities

Distribute paper and pencils. Set your alarm for about three minutes and have the kids make a list of things they need to do or will do during the next month. These things can be as small as brushing their teeth every day, or as big as graduating from high school. When the alarm goes off, the pencils stop.

Set the alarm for another three minutes (adjust as needed for your group). Have kids cross off things that really they have no choice about (attending school or needing to eat or sleep). From the items left, have kids number their top five priorities, with one being the most important.

When the alarm sounds, have them take a poll in small groups to see which were the most popular priorities.

Say: **One of the best things that happens when we set our priorities is that we have to decide what our life is really about.** Have each group report their top five priorities, and then ask: **Judging by these priorities, what is your life about?** (Being a student, being an athlete, being a son or daughter, being a musician.) **Is this what you want to be the focus or your life?** (Help kids sort through a balance between what they know they need—education, for instance—as well as other values they want reflected in their lives.) **Once we know what our life is about, we know what to make a priority and what to say no to.**

4 Observe Jesus

Jesus knew what His life was about. He knew how to set His priorities. What do you think His life was about? Have someone read Luke 19:10. **This was Jesus' statement of focus. From it, He could make His daily decisions about how to spend His time.**

- **What does "seeking and saving the lost" mean for Christ?**
- **As Christians (little Christs) what is our statement of focus?**
- **How does this affect how we spend our time?**

Have someone read Mark 1:35. **Because Jesus knew what His life was about, He knew His priority was to stay in tune with God and His plans.**

- **What did Jesus do to get in tune with God?**
- **How much time does it take to get in tune with God?**
- **What kinds of priorities must we set to be in tune with God?**

Have someone read Mark 2:15-17.

- **What was Jesus saying no to?**
- **What kinds of things do we have to say no to?**
- **What makes it hard to say no to certain people and certain things?**

5 Practice Saying No

Ask two volunteers to roleplay this situation: Youth #1 is enlisting people to help with the car wash on Saturday. Youth #2 didn't help last time because of a band contest. (He's working on a music scholarship to college.) This coming Saturday there is a practice for the next contest. Youth #1 really puts the pressure on to get Youth #2 to come to the car wash. Have the two debate both sides of the issues.

After the roleplay, ask the group:

- **Were Youth #1's arguments good ones?**
- **Should Youth #2 have gone to the car wash? Why or why not?**
- **What were each of person's priorities?**

Ask group members to suggest situations in which they must say no, then set up several role plays based on those situations.

6 Offer Accountability

Allow some quiet time in which kids can decide if they are too busy and need to say no to some things in order to keep their priorities straight. If you have an accountability structure already set up, ask them to be accountable to someone for the changes they need to make.

Ask for volunteers to share what they plan to do about their priorities.

Optional Extras

1. *Fast-Motion Skit*. Have groups of kids develop a skit showing a typical teen's weekday in fast motion—really fast motion. Give them some time to get some props and make-do costumes, if needed, then have each group perform its skit for the large group.
2. *Time Log*. Challenge kids to keep a diary of their time for a week. Use this to find out what their pressures and priorities are.

DATE USED

I'm Sinking at School

BIG IDEA

When we are sinking at school, we have to discover what is dragging us down, and then find a way to rise above it.

BIBLE INPUT

Romans 12:3-6a
Proverbs 6:1-11
Proverbs 20:4
I Corinthians 10:31

BRING:

Bible
Pencils
Paper
Flotation device (life jacket, inflatable ring, etc.)

1 Don't Get Dragged Down

Run some relay races in which some team members are "dead weight". One way to do this is to have one person race with a team member hanging onto each of his ankles. Another way is to station the team members between start and finish. They must hook up with each other as they go along, but no more than three can be bearing their weight. Try different variations on this theme, making sure each time that the group is carrying or dragging some members.

Use your flotation device as a marker for the races.

In what situations is being weighted down a plus? (Scuba divers wear weights to sink to the bottom; fishermen put weights on their lines; exercisers wear weights to strengthen muscles; hot air balloons need weights sometimes to stay down; etc.)

When is being weighted down a negative? (Learning to swim; running sprints; riding a bike.)

Say something like: **If you feel like you are sinking at school, or anywhere else, for that matter, you are being weighted down and it is hurting you. You need to figure out what's holding you down, and then make a plan to do something about it.**

2 Describe the Feeling

Stand in a large circle. Have the group pass around the flotation device. Cover your eyes for a few seconds, then say, "Stop!" Whoever is holding the float must answer out loud the following question: **"Sometimes I feel like I'm sinking in the sea of ________."** (Relationships, academics, geometry, mid-terms, sports, extra-curricular activities, family issues.)

Repeat the process until many have shared. If your group is large, do this in small groups.

3 Diagnose the Problem

Let's diagnose the problem. Why do we sometimes feel like we're sinking in school?

Distribute paper and pencils and have the group write these options down the left side of the page.

too hard
too much
too lazy
too behind

too little/too easy
too bored
Discuss what each of these diagnoses may mean in practical terms. For instance, too hard may mean being in accelerated classes when you shouldn't be. Too late may mean being a procrastinator. Too little may mean not being in accelerated classes when you should be. Ask for anything to add to the list.

4 Plan Some Solutions

Add the following passages beside the diagnoses. Give kids time to look up the Scriptures and write a one-sentence solution to the problem, starting with, "If I'm sinking in school because it is/I am too ______, then I should . . . ." Examples of possible solutions are in parentheses.

- too hard—Romans 12:3-6a (If I'm sinking at school because it is too hard, then I should be more realistic about my abilities and learn to accept not being in the advanced classes.)
- too much—Proverbs 6:1-5 (If I'm sinking in school because it is too much, then I should determine what commitments I can get out of and trim my life down to what I can manage.)
- too lazy—Proverbs 6:6-11 (If I'm sinking in school because I am too lazy, then I should get my rear in gear, take some study courses, and do what it takes to start getting some work done.)
- too behind—Proverbs 20:4 (If I'm sinking in school because I am too behind, I should cancel some activities till I catch up, see if I can get extensions on some projects, and hope for mercy from some teachers.)
- too little/too easy/too bored—I Corinthians 10:31 (If I'm sinking in school because it is too easy or I'm too bored, I should take my performance more seriously, take harder classes, and get more out of my school experience.)

Say something like: **The hard thing about feeling like we're sinking (another way to say it is feeling overwhelmed) is that we become so down or so frantic that we can't think clearly about what is really holding us down. Once we can figure that out we can make a plan.**

After the kids have written a solution for each problem, have them circle the problem that they have the most trouble with. Then have them turn over the sheet and write three things that they can do to get their head more above water. Encourage them to ask others for suggestions if they get stuck.

5 Get Real with Each Other

Ask the group to sit quietly and ask God for help in keeping their lives on an even keel. Then have them go to someone to confess how they are sinking and what they are going to do about it.

They may pray together if they want, or they may just talk. The person who is confessing should give the other person the freedom to ask about the problem the next time they see each other.

Gather the group around the flotation device, and close in prayer, asking God to help all of you to keep your heads above water.

Optional Extras

1. *Reach Out and Touch Someone*. Establish a telephone support system for those who feel like they are sinking. Form prayer partners or just make a list of those who are willing to be called on for support. Copy and distribute that list before you leave.

2. *Tutorial Tips*. Have tutor or someone in your local school district come and talk about maximizing study time. Have them give practical solutions that can help the kids dig out of a sinking spot in school.

3. *Sink or Swim Party*. Host a pool party. In permanent ink, write some of the "weights" of school on large beach balls. Let your kids blow off some steam by trying to hold the beach balls under water and being buoyed by them rather than dragged down by them.

DATE USED

I'm Discriminated Against

BIG IDEA

Discrimination hurts everybody. We need to discover the most effective ways to change discriminatory situations and survive those that can't be changed.

BIBLE INPUT

Exodus 2:11-15
Psalm 17:1-14
Acts 23:12-22
Genesis 37:1-33; 50:19-21

BRING:

Bible
Pencils
Paper
Package of colored markers

1 Simulate Discrimination

As the group members arrive, use markers to make a colored square on the back of each person's hand. After everyone is marked, explain that each color has one color it doesn't like. (Greens don't like reds, reds don't like blues, and so forth.) Then give them a task to perform (building a pyramid, rearranging the furniture, distributing refreshments, whatever) while discriminating against the color they don't like. As an option you can pick just one color that everyone will discriminate against, or divide the room into two mutually discriminatory factions.

2 Identify Our Differences

Distribute pencils and paper and have kids pair up. Give them one minute to discover as many differences as they can about each other.

When the minute is up, have them count the differences and share any unusual ones with the whole group.

Some of our differences are funny, some are interesting, and some don't make any difference at all. But in some cases, differences become the basis for discrimination between people.

Form small groups to discuss these questions:

• **Is it wrong to notice differences?** (Certainly it is important to be able to tell the difference between a red light and a green one, etc.)

• **How about differences between people? Is it better to be color-blind, or "age- blind" or "religion-blind" about people?**

• **What would be a specific example of being discriminated against?**

• **What are some differences people discriminate over?** (Race, gender, type of clothes, financial status.)

• **Have you ever felt discriminated against? How did it feel?** Allow kids to share their experiences and feelings, and encourage others to ask questions of clarification. Or, if your group does not share any experiences: **How would you feel if a close friend were discriminated against?**

• **How do you feel when you hear about these experiences of discrimination?**

3 Explore Some Case Studies

Ask volunteers to read aloud the case studies which follow, then discuss these three points of each case:

• **Is the main character correct in feeling he or she is being discriminated against?**

- **What are their choices in how to respond?**
- **What are their chances of changing the negative attitudes around them?**

CASE 1: Kent was up for a promotion at the fast-food restaurant where he worked. He had been there longer than any of the other servers. Yet when it came time for reviews and promotions, Juan was offered the position. Later Kent heard that the store had a quota on the percentage of minorities at each level of positions. Kent felt discriminated against for *not* being a minority!

CASE 2: Sarah doesn't think of it in terms of discrimination, she just knows it hurts. In her youth group most of the kids are from wealthy families. Sarah's family is just getting by. She's able to dress in style, but not with the name brands. The other girls sometimes include her in conversation at church, but they don't ever invite her shopping with them or to their slumber parties. The worst part is they talk about these excursions in front of her. They even laugh sometimes and point out other girls in the youth group who can't dress quite right. They never say anything directly to her, but Sarah wonders what they say about her when she's not around.

CASE 3: James had attended school with white kids all of his life. Even though he didn't like being the sole spokesperson for every African American, he gave the kids and teachers credit for trying to understand what it was like for blacks in America. He thought things were cool, especially when he was elected to escort the homecoming queen to the game and dance. But instead of remaining cool, several parents became really hot about a "black boy" escorting one of their girls. The parents put so much pressure on the principal that she finally told James he had to step down from the court. She was really sorry, but James understood didn't he? He didn't want to ruin homecoming, but James was furious. He blew up at the principal and stormed out of school.

4 Discover Possible Responses

Either as a whole group or in discussion groups, read these Scriptures and answer the questions below for each.

What form of discrimination did this person witness or experience?
What was his response to it?
What is your reaction to his response?
What did his response accomplish?
What do you think he wanted it to accomplish?
Can you think of a better response on his part?
How might a similar situation happen today?

- Exodus 2:11-15 (Moses took matters into his own hands.)
- Psalm 17:1-14 (David asked God to take care of it.)
- Acts 23:12-22 (Paul went to the authorities to deal with it.)
- Genesis 37:1-33; 50:19-21 (Joseph forgave.)

5 Be Quiet

Have the group think through the following questions:

• Are you using the accusation of discrimination as a way of hiding from some truth you need to face? In other words, are you sure the discrimination you feel is reality?

• Is there an authority you can go to for representation?

• Can you personally stand up against the one who is discriminating against you?

• Is it worth the fight?

• Is the discrimination happening in significant places in your life?

• What response will be the best for your long-term survival in the situation?

Let kids share their frustrations and ask for support or suggestions if they wish, but don't force sharing.

6 Down with Discrimination

Distribute paper and markers. Have them design logos for a "Stop Discrimination" campaign. Post the logos around the room and talk about ways to carry the campaign into their own lives.

In closing, go around the group and pray sentence prayers, asking God to help each of you confront discrimination in healthy, God-pleasing ways.

Optional Extras

1. *Seuss's Sneetches*. Read the Dr. Seuss book *The Star-Bellied Sneetches* with the group. Pass it around and let the kids take turns reading, then discuss how the plight of the sneetches finds a parallel in today's world.

2. *Real Case Studies*. Invite a social worker from the welfare board to talk about real and false discrimination in the cases he or she has seen.

DATE USED

I Know I Shouldn't Be Prejudiced, But . . .

BIG IDEA

If we can learn to value differences in others, we are one step closer to stopping prejudice in our own lives.

BIBLE INPUT

James 2:1-13
Acts 11:1-18
Galatians 3:26-29
Colossians 3:9-11
Romans 10:12-13
Acts 10:27-43

BRING:

Bible
Pencils
Paper

1 Play Charades

Divide into teams. Assign each team a culture or nationality (or let them think of nationalities on their own). One player must act out that culture well enough for the rest of the group to guess their nationality. If you want ,you can allow them to do "sounds like" but try to discourage it. The purpose of the activity is to identify stereotypes or obvious traits of cultures.

Some suggestions:

- Asian
- Alaskan
- Spanish
- Mexican
- Polish
- German
- American
- African American
- Russian
- Native American

You might also consider using groups at school:

- jocks
- cheerleaders
- teacher's pets
- nerds
- hoods
- preppies

Afterward, ask:

Were some of the clues you used based on stereotypes of the people? Make sure kids know you are not accusing them; point out that most people are aware of certain stereotypes or common traits of different nationalities or cultures, so that is the easiest way to identify them.

Which groups were the hardest to act out? Why? Which were the easiest? (Some groups have more identifying characteristics than others; some are seen in more stereotypical ways.)

Were you embarrassed by any of the clues you or others used? Would you have been embarrassed if someone of that race or nationality were here watching you perform?

2 Practice Classifying

Point out that in our world we are driven to classify things. Ask what classifications are used in biology, science, music, shop, English, and other school subjects.

What is the value of classifying things? (Helps us see relationships; if we understand one thing, we have a head start on understanding something similar to it.)

How does it help us understand the world better? (We can apply what we know about a category in general to each specific item in the category without having to start from scratch.)

What are some dangers in classifying things? (We can overlook the differences between individual items in a category; we can assume we know about all of them if we know about one of them.)

How do we classify people? (By race, gender, ability, interest, personality, etc.)

In what ways does that help us in our relationships? (We can be sensitive to likes and dislikes, needs, interests.)

In what ways can it hurt us in our relationships? (We don't let people out of the categories we perceive they belong in.)

How does prejudice relate to classifying people? (When we judge someone based on a general classification by race, etc., without finding out what the person is really like, we are revealing our prejudice.)

What makes it easy to be prejudiced? (Hearing stereotypes; not knowing anybody of a certain race; experiences that seem to confirm stereotypes.)

What makes it hard to know when you're prejudiced?

Point out during the discussion that classifying or stereotyping is a way we come to understand basic differences. Prejudice begins when we start to see any individual as no more than the stereotype of their larger group.

3 Explore Racism in Scripture

Divide into work groups. Give each group one of the assignments below.

• Read James 2:1-13. Make up and act out a modern-day version of this account. You may want to have someone reading the Scripture while you pantomime, or have an actual skit.

• The Jews and Gentiles had the racial skirmishes of Bible days. One of the biggest differences between Jews and Gentiles was that the Jews were circumcised and the Gentiles were not. Another big difference was that the Jews followed strict dietary laws about what they could and could not eat. The Gentiles had no such strict codes. Read Acts 11:1-18. Decide on an answer that both the Gentiles and the Jews might give to the question, "Are you prejudiced?" Start your answer with "I don't like to think of myself as prejudiced, but I don't like the way. . . ."

• Keep in mind that the terms "Greek" and "Gentile" are used interchangeably in these Scriptures. Keep in mind also that the Jews and Gentiles were two racial groups with great potential for prejudice. Read Galatians 3:26-29; Colossians 3:9-11; Romans 10:12-13. Write two letters—one from God to the Jews and Greeks about His attitude toward their prejudice, and another from God to your youth group addressing *your* prejudices.

• Peter was a prejudiced man. The way God changed his mind is found in Acts 10:27-43. After reading the passage together, write out Peter's testimony as he might tell it to your youth group.

Come back together and share the assignments.

4 *Pray and Confess*

Stand in a "hugged-up" circle (arms around each other's shoulders). Close your eyes. Have group members imagine that the people beside them are those who have been the objects of their prejudice. Have them squeeze tight as a gesture to be rid of some of that prejudice and allow these people to be treated as individuals.

Pray for God's insight and grace in dealing with prejudice. Close your prayer time by reading together Psalm 139:1-4, 23-24.

Optional Extras

1. ◆ *Ethnic Feast*. Have a dinner with multi-cultural foods. Either assign kids to bring different foods or divide them in groups, give them a nationality, and have them get take-out food for the group. Either way, encourage kids to bring things to add to the festivity—chop sticks, pinata, etc. After dinner discuss what made the foods different and what the meals had in common (they each had a main starch, some of the same meats, etc.). Brainstorm reasons that most people are drawn to the familiar.

2. ◆ *Music*. Use Twila Paris' recording of "Search My Heart" during a quiet time as you close to remind your group to let God bring to light their hidden prejudice.

DATE USED

I'm Afraid I Don't Act Like a "Real" Guy (Girl)

BIG IDEA

We don't need to let stereotypes about how men and women should act make us doubt who we are. Our gender is created by God, not by how we measure up to society's roles for men and women.

BIBLE INPUT

Genesis 1:26-28, 31
Genesis 2:4-23
Romans 1:26, 27
I John 3:16-24

BRING:

Bible
Pencils
Paper

1 Girl Talk and Guy Talk

Choose a group of guys and a group of girls to come to the front for a roleplay. Ask the boys to roleplay how girls talk about guys. Then ask the girls to roleplay the opposite. Allow the group to evaluate each performance for authenticity.

2 Create a Gender-specific Object

Distribute pencils and paper. Explain what gender-specific means (something associated with one gender specifically). Explain gender, if necessary. Ask each group member to draw, tear, fold, or mutilate the paper into one gender-specific thing. Have them show their creations to the people around them. Then have volunteers share with the whole group.

3 Identify Gender Specifics

Divide guys and girls into separate groups and have each group make up a list of:

- 5 careers that seem female-related
- 5 careers that seem male-related
- 5 guy kinds of activities
- 5 girl kinds of activities
- 5 physical traits that are gender-related (gestures or body characteristics)
- 5 male stereotypes (guys are always supposed to be . . .)
- 5 female stereotypes (girls are always supposed to be . . .)
- 5 words that describe someone who doesn't act the typical way for his or her gender
- 5 reasons they enjoy the gender they are
- 5 reasons they think it would be nice to be the opposite gender

Come back together and have one girl and one guy share the findings of his or her small group. Allow for discussion after each list.

Ask questions such as:

- **Who teaches us what is normal for a person of a specific gender to do?** (Parents, friends, TV, movies.)
- **Why does it bother us when someone doesn't stay within what we perceive as the norm for their gender?**
- **How does it feel when you do some things you aren't sure are the norm?**

4 Dramatize Scripture

Ask a narrator to read Genesis 2:4-23. As the narrator comes to any part that could be acted out (whether it be the part of God, Adam, the four rivers, or the animals) stop him or her and choose someone to take part, no matter how unexpected or even silly it might appear to be. Ask kids to be creative in their acting.

After the reading, go back and focus on the verses that have to do with the first man and woman specifically.

- **Why did God put man in a garden?** (vs. 15)
- **Why did God put woman in the garden?** (vs. 18)
- **Where did God look first for a suitable companion?** (vs. 19)

Read Genesis 1:26-28.

- **What did God want the man and woman to do?**
- **Why do you think God made the genders different?**
- **What are some ways men's and women's differences work well together?**

5 Discuss Homosexuality

Say something like: **The issue of homosexuality has made us all worry a lot more about whether we are "normal" for our gender. Your sexuality is more than how you feel about the opposite sex. You are a man because you have male genitals and chromosomes, not because you don't hold your hand limp at the wrist. You are a woman because you have female reproductive organs, whether or not you played with dolls or trucks as a child.**

Ask:

- **How is the world different now that homosexuality is an open and hot topic?**
- **What kinds of questions or feelings about your sexuality do people have that you don't think people three generations ago had?**
- **Do you think when your parents were teenagers they ever worried about whether they acted appropriately for their gender?**
- **What are some words we use to describe a person who does things that seem out of character for his or her gender?** (Tomboy, sissy, pantywaist, butch, gay.)

Before you read Romans 1:26, 27, point out that it is one of the most well-known passages used against the practice of homosexuality. After you read it, say something like this: **There are many things in our world that are a reality. We can't pretend they don't exist. But we need to know that they are not the way God designed the world to be. This passage describes homosexual practice as one of those things.**

Ask questions to discern your group's hot buttons regarding homosexuality. Focus on their specific concerns.

6 Define Normal

As a group, make a list of things for which we keep track of averages (average inches of rainfall, average height, average weight, batting average). Say: **It seems like we're always looking for the norm, some standard to compare ourselves by.**

Point out that few people are actually average. Encourage your teens to remember that they are valuable creations of God. He made each person a unique design, not a statistic for a national average. Girl or guy, they are OK just as they are, because that's how God created them. Your kids can trust God and find their worth and identity in Him.

We worry so much sometimes about the average, or the "norm," but we need to remember that God, not society or our peers, is our judge. His opinion is what matters. Read I John 3:16-24. **Even when we doubt or feel bad about ourselves, we must remember that God created us and gave us His Spirit. God is greater than any opinion, even our own.**

Optional Extras

1. *Saturday Morning Roles*. Record some Saturday morning children's programs (and commercials). As your kids watch the video, have them look for examples that reinforce stereotypes of what boys like and what girls like. For example, the color blue for boys and pink for girls; G.I. Joe and Barbie; the frightened and squeamish girl and the adventurous brave boy.

2. *Referral*. This session focuses on helping heterosexual teenagers overcome labels and gender stereotypes. Some of your kids might be struggling with their sexual orientation. You might want to get the name of a professional counselor. Also, a good book to recommend is *A Safe Place* by Jan Morrison (published by Harold Shaw Publishers, Wheaton, Illinois.) While the book is about sexual abuse, it does have good information about one's sexual identity.

DATE USED

I Can't Cheer Up

BIG IDEA

If you can't cheer up, your emotions are telling you there's a problem. To really cheer up you'll have to deal with the problem.

BIBLE INPUT

Ephesians 4:22-24
Isaiah 61:3
John 16:33
I Thessalonians 4:16-18
II Corinthians 1:3, 4

BRING:

Bible
Pencils
Paper
Bandana or blindfold

1 Blind Man's Obstacle Course

Set up a simple obstacle course using chairs or people as the obstacles. Choose one person to "run" the course and blindfold him or her. (After you blindfold him or her, change a few things in the course so he or she can't do it from memory.)

Before your blind person starts the course, have the group begin a quiet droning of continuous "beep-beep-beeps." This noise is the blind person's warning system. The louder the beeps get, the closer he or she is to an obstacle.

The group should help him or her get all the way through the course without touching any obstacles. Repeat as many times as it is fun for your group.

2 Emotions As Warning Signals

In many ways, our bodies function just like those beeps in our game. Our bodies helps us interpret what is around us.

One way is through our nerve endings. When we cut or bruise ourselves, we feel—what? Pain. Our body sends a message.

Our senses are another way our body helps us interpret the world around us. We feel heat before it burns us. We smell something we love to eat before we dig in.

Our emotions are another way that our body helps us interpret the world around us. When we are wronged we feel anger. When we lose something we feel sad.

Ask:

What could have happened if the blind man in our obstacle course had covered his ears and not listened to the warning signals?

What could happen if we had no sense of feeling and leaned up against a hot stove?

What could happen if we feel really bad emotionally and we just ignore it?

What could our emotions be telling us about our world if we feel scared? (We are in danger.) **Happy?** (We feel completely safe.) **Confused?** (We are getting mixed messages.) **Sad?** (We have lost something important to us.)

Sometimes we call not being able to cheer up "having the blues."

What does it feel like to have the blues? How does someone act who has the blues?

What other words do we use to describe someone who can't cheer up? (Sad, depressed.)

What are some circumstances that give someone the blues? (Not getting something you want, someone dies, something bad happens, it rains.)

3 Walk the Walk

Ask several volunteers to show how people walk when they feel happy, sad, sick, elated. Then have several people read aloud, showing the way someone talks who feels happy, sad, sick, or elated.

Read the first half of Proverbs 15:30. Ask: **Do you think it's easier to act yourself into a new way of feeling, or to feel yourself into a new way of acting?** Point out that one way to start cheering up is to start acting like you feel better. Start walking your happy walk, instead of your sad walk.

4 Match Life with Scriptures

Have the group write down the following reasons for feeling blue.

- Something about our life has changed, and we can't figure out what to do about it.
- We are unhappy about something in our life and it will never change.
- We have gotten in the habit of being down, and just forget to cheer up.
- We just get tired of the bad things we see around us in life.

Break into groups and have the groups decide which passage from the list below might be a comfort to a person in each of the situations listed above. Ask what a person in each situation could do to comfort himself, and what his friends could do to comfort him.

- Ephesians 4:22-24
- John 16:33
- Isaiah 61:3
- I Thessalonians 4:16-18
- II Corinthians 1:3, 4

If you have any extra time in small groups, add to the list of discouraging situations and see if you can find Scriptures to comfort people in those situations.

5 Make Happy Plans

On the reverse side of the paper, have group members list things that make them feel good—activities, places, people, foods, ideas, etc.

Encourage them to keep this list and to do some of these things or call some of these people when they feel down.

6 Share with Each Other

One of the best ways to cheer up is to tell someone else how you're feeling. Have the group break into twos or threes and share something they are or have been down about.

Have someone read Romans 12:15 and II Corinthians 1:3, 4. Hold up the handkerchief you used earlier. Encourage your group to be a comfort to each other when they are down. Have everyone gather round. If possible, have each person grab onto the handkerchief (this gets the group *really* close). Close in prayer.

Optional Extras

1. *Guest Resource.* Invite a psychologist to come for a Q & A session about teenage depression.

2. *Peer Counseling Program.* Set up a peer counseling program among your group. Your program can be as simple as phone numbers listed in an order so that a prayer request for someone can be circulated around the group quickly (some call this a prayer chain). Or you can actually choose and train peer counselors who commit themselves to being available for others in the group during down or difficult times.

3. *Dumb Joke Contest.* Announce the first and last annual dumb joke contest. Anyone can enter. The rules are simple: only dumb jokes allowed. Give kids a few minutes to think up some incredibly dumb jokes. Kids should run their jokes by you for approval (censor only the off-color or dirty ones). When a contestant tells his or her joke, the rest of the group responds with groans, boos, and hisses. The winner of the contest is the one who received the loudest groans. You might want to come up with a gag award for the winner. Here's one to get you started: Why don't the blue gills like to play baseball? Because it's three strikes and your trout!

DATE USED

I'm So Uncoordinated!

BIG IDEA

We need to learn to give ourselves a break when we do uncoordinated things that embarrass us. And we need to do the same for others when they trip up.

BIBLE INPUT

Ephesians 4:32
Romans 15:7
Colossians 3:12, 13
Joel 2:13
Ecclesiastes 7:8

BRING:

Bible
Pencils
Paper

1 It Takes Coordination

As you begin the session, trip or do something uncoordinated. Take note of any comments kids make. Say something like: **OK, let's see how coordinated we are.** Quickly call out one coordination task after another for kids to do—rubbing head while patting stomach and vice versa, hopping on left foot while doing the twist. Make it hard enough that everyone messes up and everyone laughs.

2 Coordinate a Group

Divide the group in two. Call one group to the front. Say: **You have 25 seconds to form a human pyramid. You may not talk while you're doing it.** Watch them scramble.

Call the second group to the front. Say: **You have 20 seconds to discuss procedure, then 25 seconds to form a human pyramid.**

Compare how the experiences differed. (The second group should have an easier time of it.) Point out that the second group had time to coordinate. The first group didn't.

What does it mean to be coordinated? (Your body can organize itself to accomplish complicated as well as simple tasks.) **So what does it mean to be the opposite?**

What are some activities that require coordination? (Balance beam, ice skating, some dancing, some cheerleading, basketball.)

What does it feel like to do something uncoordinated? (Refer to the experience everyone has probably had of tripping on carpet when there's nothing there to trip on. What does everyone do? Look behind you to see what grabbed your foot.)

How do we usually respond when someone does something uncoordinated?

Discuss slapstick comedy—humor built on uncoordination and human pain. Talk about why it is funny to see someone tripping all over himself. Point out that it feels different laughing at someone than being laughed at for being uncoordinated.

If you're uncoordinated as a teenager, will you be all your life? Discuss the tendency in adolescence to be uncoordinated. Cite body changes and growth spurts as some reasons that the body can't organize itself as well. Assure kids that being clumsy or uncoordinated as an adolescent doesn't mean you will always be.

In what other ways do we embarrass ourselves, besides being uncoordinated?

What is it like to feel embarrassed?

What is it like to see others embarrass themselves?

How can we help someone when he or she is embarrassed?

What can we do for ourselves when we are embarrassed?

3 Play Charades on Paper

Distribute pencils and paper. Play in small groups or with the whole group. Assign the following words for someone in the group to draw (no talking allowed!) so the group can guess: drop, choke, spit, fall, trip, stumble, slip, tumble. The words are related to uncoordinated things we do to embarrass ourselves.

4 Apply Scriptures

Some of the greatest kindnesses that we can show each other are in embarrassing situations. And many embarrassing situations result when we do uncoordinated things.

Have volunteers read aloud the following three Scriptures: Romans 15:7; Ephesians 4:32; Colossians 3:12, 13. Ask the following questions:

- **List the positive ways we as Christians should treat people.**
- **What's the basis for accepting people, forgiving them, and putting up with them?** (We have received God's forgiveness and acceptance.)
- **How does God treat us?** Have someone read Joel 2:13. Mention that we don't deserve God's kindness or compassion. We were the ones that sinned, but God loves us and wants us to have a right relationship with Him.

Have someone read Ecclesiastes 7:8. **Put this verse into your own words so it applies to embarrassing situations.**

5 Write a Letter

Read aloud the following letters.

Dear Friend,

I have a problem. I am always embarrassing myself in one way or another. If I'm not falling, I'm tripping. If I'm not tripping, I'm dropping something.

Usually I try to just pass it off or look around real mean to warn everyone around me not to laugh. Is that the best response?

Signed,
Too Embarrassed to Look

Dear Counselor,

I am miserable. During the last year my feet grew two sizes! It's like I can't navigate on them any more! What's going to happen to me? Am I ever going to be able to walk a straight line?

Please tell me it'll be OK.

Signed,
Barely Standing

Have each group write a letter in response to one of the letters above. Encourage them to use some of the passages you just discussed.

When most people have finished, ask for volunteers to share their correspondence. Close in prayer, thanking God for His acceptance and compassion. Ask His help in treating others the same way, especially in embarrassing situations.

Optional Extras

1. *Slapstick Starter*. Show a slapstick comedy to open the session. Try an episode of "The Three Stooges" or "The Dick Van Dyke Show," or part of a Marx Brothers movie.

2. *Crazy Coordination*. Make up a crazy, difficult dance that no one could ever do well and teach it during the session to "test" coordination.

3. *Jenga*. Play the game, Jenga, if you have one available. Kids take turns removing small blocks of wood with one hand and stacking the blocks on top of the rest. It's a real test of of coordination. Each time a block is removed, have the person who removed it share a time he or she was embarrassed or did something uncoordinated.

DATE USED

I Can't Get Along With . . .

BIG IDEA

We will always find people who rub us the wrong way, but we honor God when we work to get along with our least favorite people.

BIBLE INPUT

Romans 12:17-21
Romans 15:7
I John 4:7, 8

BRING:

Bible
Pencils
Paper
Long rope or cord

1 Rate Pet Peeves

Read aloud the following list of irritating traits or pet peeves. Have the kids make a sound like a buzzer on a game show. The more the item irritates them, the louder the buzz should be.

- **Someone talking with a mouth full of food**
- **Someone calling you "honey" or "sweetie" all the time**
- **Someone putting his or her retainer beside his or her plate at lunch**
- **Someone copying everything you do**
- **Someone flirting with every guy/girl she/he talks to**
- **Someone interrupting you all the time**
- **Someone always picking his or her teeth**
- **Someone always picking his nose**
- **Someone running fingernails down a chalkboard**
- **Someone making you play silly games during youth group**

Next have individuals volunteer their pet peeves. See who can find the most disgusting one that evokes the loudest response from the group.

2 Define Not Getting Along

Divide the group in half. Have one side complete the statement, "Getting along with someone feels like . . ." in five different ways. Have the other side complete the statement, "Not getting along with someone means . . ." in five different ways.

When they are finished formulating their statements, have the teams read their statements.

3 Play Tug of War

Divide into two teams and play a game of tug of war. Place some object on the floor at the middle of the rope. The first group to pull the other past that object wins. Play several times.

Spread the rope across the front of the class, at eye level if possible.

Say: **When we are not getting along with someone, it is a constant tug of war. We are pulling in opposite directions.**

Write "My Way" on two pieces of paper and attach each to an end of the rope. **When we are not getting along with someone, usually we have lost sight of the relationship and we are both trying to get our own way.**

In order to quit our game of tug of war, we need to learn to negotiate. That

means we set a common goal (such as having a happy relationship) instead of working toward opposite goals (such as getting our own way).

4 Identify Steps to Negotiating

Write the steps to negotiating (below) on pieces of paper and hang them on the rope (you can use tape or paper clips, or tear a hole in the paper and put the rope through it) as you talk about each one.

- Step #1: Establish a mutual desire to have a happy relationship.
- Step #2: Decide who will express an opinion first.
- Step #3: When the other person is expressing his or her perspective, listen completely before expressing your own.
- Step #4: Express your own perspective without accusing or name calling. Own your own feelings (not the other person's) and state specifically how you would like the relationship to be different.
- Step #5: When things get emotional, back off, and go to Step #1.
- Step #6: Ask for help in coming to a compromise if you need it.

Ask kids to walk along the rope, starting at Step #1 and stopping when they reach a step that they don't understand or that would be difficult for them. Have every person share why they stopped where they did.

5 Find Biblical Guidelines

Have someone read each of the passages below, then share opinions on the questions for each.

- Romans 12:17-21

What does this *not* give you the freedom to do when you aren't getting along with someone?

What are some specific ways that we get revenge in our group? (Ignoring people, acting catty, making someone feel excluded, playing cruel jokes.)

- Romans 15:7

How has Christ accepted us when we are disagreeable? When we ignore Him?

What makes it hard to accept each other that same way?

- I John 4:7, 8

Does God take it seriously if we don't love each other? Explain.

Say something like: **If we are not willing or even interested in getting along, then we aren't loving each other. We don't have to like everything about each other to be civil and to honor God in our relationships.**

6 Make a Circle

Tie the ends of the rope together and make a circle with everyone holding on to the rope. Have someone read John 15:9-11. Point out that you have a common goal as a group to exhibit Christ to the rest of the world by loving each other.

Optional Extras

1. *Roleplays*. Set up some common scenarios of kids not getting along and have the kids roleplay a negotiating session. Choose three kids and have one be the mediator. He or she will read each step and the other two will act it out. The mediator has the right and the responsibility to stop the other two if they break the rules (such as speaking while the other person is expressing his perspective).

   Here are a couple of situations to get you started. Situation 1: Jenny and Laura had a major fight. Laura went out with the guy Jenny liked. And Laura didn't even have the decency to tell Jenny. But why should she? Jenny wasn't dating the guy. Situation 2: When Dylan asked his small group to pray for Brent's sister who was pregnant and not married, Dylan had no idea Brent would blow up at him. Brent insists that Dylan broke a confidence. Dylan just wanted to help.

2. *Fake Fights*. Stage some mock fights. Pick three or four pairs before your meeting and give them roles to play (friends, siblings, parent/child, dates). Have them prepare a mock fight to open class. Their fight should last less than two minutes and each person should be able to state his side of it. For fun, act out the fights in super slow motion. Afterward, ask kids for suggestions for negotiating the disagreement.

DATE USED

I Can't Get a Date

BIG IDEA

Whether you are dating or not, you can still have a good time and feel good about the person God created you to be.

BIBLE INPUT

John 3:16
Romans 5:8
I John 3:1
I John 3:16

BRING:

Bible
Pencils
Paper

1 A Game of Groups and Pairs

Tell kids to form groups of whatever number you call, trying to be the first group formed each time. Start with a big number and make your way down to two.

You can play with elimination—anyone not in the right number group is eliminated. Or you can leave everyone in all the time and just switch around the groups.

After the game is over, point out: **This game reflects one way of dating. You don't have to start out with just two people. The groups you go out with can vary. Eventually you can settle down to a pair. But you don't have to have a pair to have a good time.**

Ask:

What is difficult about not having a steady date?

What are some activities or places where you feel left out without a date?

What is the purpose of dating? (Finding a mate, having a good time, getting out, being popular.)

If you see the purpose of dating as having a good time, do you have to be in a couple to have a good time?

2 Perceptions about Dating

Divide into discussion groups and have the groups complete these sentences in as many different ways as they can.

- Some people believe if you don't have a date it's because. . . .
- Some people believe if you go out with a lot of people it means you. . . .
- Some people believe if you go out with the same person all the time it means. . . .

Before you have the groups come back together, have them write three plans for group dates. When you come back together, collect the group date ideas, but let each group report how it finished the sentences.

3 Paraphrase How God Sees Us

Say something like: **We receive so many messages telling us what we need to be to be worth something. Some say we must be good-looking, some say we must be paired off, some say we must have certain kinds of careers or a certain amount of money.**

We need to know for sure who we are and what we are worth so that we are not blown away by all the messages we receive.

Have different people read aloud the Scriptures below. After each one, have the group write in their own words God's opinion of them as shown in the passage.

- John 3:16
- Romans 5:8
- I John 3:1
- I John 3:16

The obvious answer is that God loves us, which He does. But there's a lot more to God's love. Mention that God's love is unconditional. His love is constant and consistent. It's not based on anything we do or on who we are. In fact, Romans 5:8 essentially says that God proved His love for us when we were at our worst, that is, sinners, by sending His Son to die for us. That old familiar verse, John 3:16, reminds us of the sacrifice God made: He gave us His one and only Son.

God squanders His love on us. He wants us to become His children and have eternal life. Does God feel this way only if we're dating someone? (Of course not.) Stress that the only thing our dating status is an indicator of is—our dating status.

Ask: **Even though we know God loves us, why do we sometimes feel bad if we don't have a date?** Give kids a chance to express their feelings. It's hard not to feel as if something is wrong with you when you don't date. Again, emphasize that a person's true worth and value come from God.

Bring the discussion around to the things that guys and girls can do to make themselves fun people to be with. (For example, practice basic personal hygiene, be relaxed, don't be obnoxious, like people, be interested in others besides yourself.) Close by saying something like: **You may not be the dating king or queen, but as long as you're doing your best and you're content with who you are, relax, have a good time, and remember that there's plenty of time for dating.**

4 Plan Group Dates

Shuffle the group date ideas from Step 2 and read them to the group. Talk about how they think each would work and whether they think it sounds fun.

If possible, make plans to carry out some of the dates.

Optional Extras

1. ◆ *Historic Dates*. Assign small groups an era of history. Have them create costumes for a couple from newspaper and portray how modern dating would have looked in that era.

Suggested eras of history:

The World's First Date	Colonial America
Greek Civilization	Bible Times
The Dark Ages	Roman Civilization
The England of Henry VIII	The 60s in America

Display the couples in a fashion show format with each group emceeing their couple as they parade around the room. Afterward point out to the group that actually until this century there was no such thing as dating. Marriages were (and still are in many cultures) arranged, and falling in love, if it happened, came much later. Get your group's impressions of *that*.

2. ◆ *Panel Discussion*. Have a panel made up of both singles and couples to discuss whether a young person needs to date in order to enjoy his or her teenage years.

DATE USED

I Don't Know What to Do with My Life

BIG IDEA

Choosing a career is important. But it's more important to commit to serving God no matter what profession we are in.

BIBLE INPUT

Psalm 37:3-7
Ecclesiastes 5:18-20
Acts 18:1-4

BRING:

Bible
Pencils
Paper
Yellow pages torn from a phone book

1 Snap Out Names of Careers

Sit in a circle. Establish a rhythm by slapping your knees twice, then clapping your hands twice, then snapping your fingers twice. As the group beats out the rhythm, go around the circle with each group member naming one career on the two finger snaps.

If you have an exceptionally bright group, have them name careers alphabetically. For instance, the first person says acrobat, the second bear trainer, and so on. (Try to arrange the seating so you don't get stuck with X or Z.)

2 Tell Tall Tales

Sometimes you come to know what to do with your life in a lightning flash. Sometimes it's just through everyday living.

Establish two teams. The first team must pick a business out of the yellow pages. The other team must then make up a story about how the person in that career discovered he or she wanted to do it. It should be the most dramatic of revelations. (Something like: Sam Edwards, podiatrist for the zoo, decided upon his career when he was stampeded by a herd of baby elephants. The footprints were left indelibly on his body.)

Have teams alternate picking the careers and telling the stories, trying to make the stories more and more outrageous each time.

3 Examine Scripture

Distribute paper and pencils. Have kids work through the following Scripture-related assignments individually, discussing each assignment before going on to the next.

• **Read Ecclesiastes 5:18-20 and write a paraphrase of this passage in 25 words or less—the less the better. What does this say about our job or life's work? What is the main message of this passage?** Ask volunteers to read their paraphrases. Point out that we do have to make a living, but it is God's gift to us to enjoy our work.

• **Read Psalm 37:3-7. Each sentence starts with a verb describing how we are to act toward God as we think about our life direction. Make a list of these verbs** (trust, delight, commit, be still) **then make a corresponding list of the ways the psalm says God will respond to your action (not every action has a response listed).** (Give you safe pasture; give you the desires of your heart; make your righteousness shine.)

Compare the lists and ask for specific examples of how your group can do these things as they search out what to do with their lives. What does it really mean for them to trust in God?

• **Read Acts 18:1-4. Finish this sentence: To "minister" is to...** Review with your group Saul/Paul's conversion and subsequent induction into ministry. Point out that while he was in "full-time ministry" he also worked for a living.

Discuss with your group the different facets of ministry/vocational ministry:

• Vocational ministry: your livelihood depends on the salary you receive from your ministry.

• Bi-vocational ministry: you have a different job to support the ministry things you do.

• Lay ministry: you minister as you go. Your job isn't necessarily ministry-related; you just minister as God gives you opportunity.

Point out to your group that all three are honorable. As Christians, though, we should fit into one category.

4 Conduct a Q & A Session

Open up an old-time jam session. Ask for any and every question regarding life direction.

If you want to make it funny, talk about the coffeehouses of the sixties and imagine you are all hippies sitting around in a coffeehouse. Instead of clapping when someone said something they liked, they snapped their fingers. Invite your group to do that, and to say "groovy" a lot to establish a nonthreatening way to loosen up and discuss.

Open the jam session with these two questions (or similar ones of your own).

• **Is it wrong to have a job where you make a lot of money?**

• **Are there any kinds of jobs that Christians shouldn't do?**

Find out what is on your group's minds about careers, their confusions, their focuses, their lack of focus. Address any issues that you can. Ask what other's opinions are on some questions. Make notes for future sessions.

5 Job Listings

Give each kid a page from the yellow pages. Have each one look over the category. (Editor's note: I was alarmed to find pages and pages of escort services. You might want to delete those from this activity.)

Remind group members that each entry involves someone who needed to know what to do with his or her life. For now, anyway, that person has found that. Your kids aren't alone in their struggle. They aren't the first or last. But their struggle is their own to fight through.

Point out that the yellow pages are a good place to think of ideas of what types of careers are available. Then point out that the pages of their Bibles also will give them direction. (Do you dare close with, "If you let your fingers do the walking"?)

Say: **Some of you already may know what you want to do with your life. If so, go for it. Others of you may not have a clue about what you want to do. If that's the case, keep your options open. Talk to people, collect information, and ask God for wisdom in choosing your career.** In closing, pray for your group, that all of them will rely on God's wisdom as they make choices and decisions about their futures.

Optional Extras

1. ◆ *Personality Profiles.* Talk with a counselor in your area about purchasing and administering a personality test to help your kids get to know themselves a little better.

2. ◆ *Library Lock-in.* Take your group to the library and do some research on their interests and careers. What periodicals or professional societies relate to their interests? Have the librarian help them know what tools are useful to their search.

3. ◆ *Career Forum.* Invite several adults to briefly describe what they do and field questions about their careers. Be sure to include a wide variety of careers: clerical, professional, hourly, stay-at-home mothers, people in a vocational ministry, and so on.

DATE USED

I'm Disappointed with God

BIG IDEA

We don't always get what we hope for, even though we know God has the power to do anything. But we can still trust God enough to be honest with Him about our disappointments.

BIBLE INPUT

Jonah 4:1-11
Job 2:7-10
Mark 15:33, 34
Psalm 44:23-26

BRING:

Bible
Pencils
Paper

1 Show How Low You Would Go

Instruct the group to respond to each of the statements below according to whether they would feel disappointed or happy about it. The more disappointed they would feel, the lower they should position themselves (with lying on the floor being the lowest) and the happier they would feel, the taller they should stand (standing tiptoe on a chair being the highest). If it doesn't affect them at all, they can stay seated.

For the statements containing ellipses (those three little dots), have kids respond to the first part before reading the second part. Add some of your own that specifically apply to your group and their interests.

- **You might get tickets to a professional football game.**
- **You might get tickets to a fashion show.**
- **Your best friend is moving when school's out.**
- **You have a date to the school dance next week.**
- **You are going to spend the evening with just you and your dad.**
- **You made third chair in the band.**
- **The school play, in which you have a minor role, has been cancelled.**
- **You find out you're going to a family reunion this weekend . . . instead of having your wisdom teeth out.**
- **You find out you're going to another family reunion next weekend . . . instead of a party at a friend's house.**

2 Discuss Disappointment

Divide into discussion groups. Have each person in the group respond to this statement: **Tell us about one time you wanted something so badly that you pretended not to want it so you wouldn't be disappointed.**

Then discuss the following questions.

What does disappointment feel like?

What kinds of things do we do to keep from feeling disappointed?

What has to happen before we can be disappointed? (We have to want, hope, or wish for something.)

Are you ever disappointed in yourself? How does that happen?

Are you ever disappointed in God? How does that happen?

Should we try to hide our feelings from God?

Do we ever have a right to be disappointed in God? Why?

How do you think our disappointment affects God?

Even though we know God doesn't always do what we ask, should we still ask? Why?

3 Disappointments in the Bible

Stay in your discussion groups. As a large group go over the introductory information on each Scripture passage. Then have each group read the Scripture and discuss the questions.

1. Jonah had run away from God and from Nineveh. But when he finally got out of the fish and went to the town, the people turned away from their sin and back to God. This is what Jonah wanted, right?

Read Jonah 4:1-11.

- What was Jonah upset about?
- What did he accuse God of?
- He was disappointed in God. What did Jonah expect of God that he didn't get?
- How did God respond to Jonah's disappointment?
- How did Jonah express his disappointment to God?
- How did God respond to that honesty?

2. Job lost everything. He had to deal with disappointment, and his wife did too. She was also disappointed with God.

Read Job 2:7-10.

- What was Job's wife's response to disappointment with God?
- What was Job's response?
- From their responses, what do you think was different about what each expected from God?

3. Jesus went to the cross to die. He was God, yet human. In His humanity He felt disappointed.

Read Mark 15:33, 34.

- What had God the Father done that Jesus didn't expect?
- Were those actions necessary?
- If we believe that, even though we are disappointed in God's actions, His actions are necessary, does that make the disappointment any easier to take?

4. The psalms are songs that David and other writers composed. They express human emotions of all kinds.

Read Psalm 44:23-26.

- What do you think this person expected from God that he hadn't gotten yet?
- What kinds of emotions was he feeling?
- Even though this writer was disappointed in God's reaction thus far, how did he express the idea that God is loving?

4 Hear a Story

One summer in the southeastern United States a man was cutting his grass with a riding lawn mower. He allowed his son to ride with him. As they cut a corner too quickly, the boy slipped and was about to plunge toward the blades. In an attempt to protect his son, the man grabbed him by the arm and threw him away from the machine. Unfortunately, the man didn't throw his son quite hard enough and the boy's foot was still caught in the blade.

Later at the hospital the boy awakened and looked in the face of his harried dad. The son's first words were, "Daddy, why did you throw me into the lawn mower?"

- How did the child's perception differ from reality?
- Was the child's perception reasonable, given his understanding?
- How could our perception of God's actions be compared to this child's reactions?
- How can we trust God even when we don't understand his actions?

5 Get Honest

Close the session with three steps for dealing with disappointment with God:

1. Go to God and honestly express your feelings.

2. Share with someone you trust that you are struggling.

3. Remind yourself that you can trust the intent of God's heart, even if you don't understand the effect of His actions.

Allow the group time to share either as a group or individually. They can share past experiences of disappointment with God or present ones.

Optional Extras

1. *Hope List.* Establish a system of sharing and keeping tabs on the things your kids are hoping for from God. It may be as simple as a prayer request list, or as involved as weekly printouts. This will show you when God comes through, but also the places where your teens can become disappointed with God.

2. *Letters to God.* Have each person write a letter to God about a disappointment. Encourage honesty in the letter, but also encourage expressing to God the recognition that He is more than just someone who does what we want. Urge kids to list specific ways in which they believe He is trustworthy.